LORD, TEACH US TO PRAY

Lord, Teach Us to Pray

A New Look at the Lord's Prayer

ARTHUR PAUL BOERS

HERALD PRESS
Waterloo, Ontario
Scottdale, Pennsylvania

Canadian Cataloguing in Publication Data
Boers, Arthur Paul, 1957-
Lord teach us to pray

Includes bibliographical references.
ISBN 0-8361-3583-0

1. Lord's prayer. I. Title.

BV230.B64 1992 226.9'606 C92-093842-6

The paper used in this publication is recycled and meets the minimum requirements of American National Standard for Information Sciences —Permanence of Paper for Printed Library Materials, ANSI Z39.48-1984.

Library of Congress Catalog Number: 92-71102
International Standard Book Number: 0-8361-3583-0
Printed in the United States of America
Cover and book design by Gwen M. Stamm/Cover photo by Paul M. Schrock from Gerald C. Studer's Bible collection

00 99 98 97 96 95 94 93 92 10 9 8 7 6 5 4 3 2 1

To Lorna . . . at last!

Contents

Preface

It is not easy to neatly dissect my life into roles of husband, father, son, preacher, and writer. Everything mixes and flows together, sometimes to the mutual advantage of all my roles and sometimes, alas, to their mutual detriment. By God's grace and with the support of many significant persons, I continue to sense God's providential movement in my life. Special thanks to a few people that here must be named.

It is a joy to work again with an editor, Michael A. King, whom I also count as a good friend. Many thanks for his support, not only of my writing, but also of me personally.

The year that Herald Press accepted this manuscript, 1991, was one of both great joys and tremendous sorrows. Betty L. Kurtz and Paul M. Schrock at Herald Press went the extra mile in making my first book available early enough to share with my terminally ill father. Words fail me.

In the publishing sphere, David Graybill of *Christian Living* and Mark R. Halton of *The Christian Ministry* have given new impetus to my writing.

My thanks to Muriel Bechtel and Lydia Harder. You both know why. Although we have differences of opinion, I gratefully esteem your insights.

The Windsor Mennonite Fellowship endured a series of sermons on the Lord's Prayer! Their endurance made this book possible.

Deep appreciation to "the breakfast club": Jim Brown of Harrow Mennonite, Edwin Epp of Faith Mennonite, Menno Epp of Leamington United Mennonite, and the North Leamington contingent of Cornie Driedger, Vic Kliewer, and James Nickel.

Wholehearted thanks to Kevin Abma, the friend who sticks closer than a brother (Prov. 18:24); Mary Stewart, our family friend; and Herb Schultz, who pastors me.

My mother, Roelie Boers, and my children, Erin Margaret and Paul Edward, are among the chief joys of my life. Many thanks.

Last and most important, I offer thanks to my dear wife, Lorna Jean McDougall. If schedules proceed as they should (never a guarantee in publishing), this will be my third book. It is high time that a volume be dedicated to her. Lorna is my dearest friend, my partner in all that is important, and a steady companion always. I will ever be grateful to and for her. May we be blessed with several more dozen years of marriage.

—Arthur Paul Boers
Ontario, Canada

Introduction

Lord Teach Us to Pray

The Lord's Prayer is well known, yet little understood. Its overexposure has hardened our hearts to its richness. It is often repeated, yet little contemplated. Unfortunately, our abuse of the Lord's Prayer has emptied it of meaning, often reducing it to the very vain repetition that Jesus warned of before he taught the Lord's Prayer in the Sermon on the Mount.

Like many of my generation, I was exposed to the Lord's Prayer early and often, hearing it repeated in many different contexts, both sacred and secular. I began to pay deeper attention to the Lord's Prayer as a pastor who was becoming more and more interested in spirituality. In Chicago, we prayed it each Sunday in both English and Spanish. At the Windsor Mennonite Fellowship, we often recited it together after the sharing of joys and concerns. Later I realized that even while I was finally appreciating this prayer, many other people were bored with what they had heard so often.

As part of exploring spirituality in the congregation, I began to preach on the Lord's Prayer. Most expected this sermon series to last two or three sessions. Many wondered what insights could be gleaned from such a familiar prayer.

Rather than preaching two or three times on the Lord's

Prayer, however, I needed a whole sermon just to introduce it. The salutation, "Our Father," required two sermons. After three sermons I had only worked on two words! (Some were amused at the length and detail of my sermons. But at this point others nervously began to calculate how many sermons it would take to preach the whole Lord's Prayer!) I myself was surprised when the prayer developed into a series of over a dozen sermons.

The Lord's Prayer: Importance in Church History

As I read significant theologians, I am struck with the importance they attributed to this prayer. Dietrich Bonhoeffer wrote,

> The Lord's Prayer is not merely the pattern prayer, it is the way Christians *must* pray. If they pray this prayer, God will certainly hear them. The Lord's Prayer is the quintessence of prayer. A disciple's prayer is founded on and circumscribed by it.[1]

Will Campbell, Baptist preacher and author, marvels at all the locations where the Lord's Prayer is cited and used.

> Coronation of queens at Westminster Abbey and revival meetings under an Appalachian brush arbor. Blessing of the shrimp fleet in Gulfport and last words uttered on the sinking Titanic. Matins at a convent school in Kenya and baccalaureate at Harvard. Blue and gray at Gettysburg. Christian killing Christian. Our Father. Ecclesia and aimless vagrants. A dying old man's baptism in a bathtub and a little girl's confirmation in San Juan. Our Father.[2]

No matter what our background, most of us know the Lord's Prayer. Until recently, it was even taught in many state-run schools throughout the United States and Canada. (Now it is at the center of raging church-state controversies about whether it is appropriate to pray the Lord's Prayer in public schools.) Most of us have learned this prayer early and heard it often.

As with most important subjects, the more we research the Lord's Prayer the less we find we know about it. Much has been written and preached on this subject. At every major point in church history, leaders worked with the Lord's Prayer. They prayed it, taught it, and preached about it. Origen, Tertullian,

Cyprian, Augustine, Thomas Aquinas, Meister Eckhart, Martin Luther, and John Calvin all wrote extensively about the Lord's Prayer.

This prayer has nourished every generation of Christians. Tertullian, a respected church father, said the Lord's Prayer was a summary of the whole gospel. In importance and influence, the Lord's Prayer ranks with the Apostles' Creed—with the added advantage that the Lord's Prayer comes mostly from the Bible, while the Apostles' Creed does not.

In the church, the Lord's Prayer has played vitally important roles in the worship of congregations and in the personal prayers of believers. Simone Weil, a great mystic, prayed the Lord's Prayer every day in deep contemplation.

> I have made a practice of saying it through once each morning with absolute attention. If during the recitation my attention wanders or goes to sleep, in the minutest degree, I begin again until I have once succeeded in going through it with absolutely pure attention.[3]

Weil was convinced that this discipline could change lives. "It is impossible to say it once through, giving the fullest possible attention to each word, without a change, infinitesimal perhaps but real, taking place in the soul."[4] Similarly, Martin Luther said, "I am convinced that when a Christian rightly prays the Lord's Prayer at any time . . . [their] praying is more than adequate."[5]

The high value so many have placed on this prayer makes me hesitant to presume to write about such an esteemed subject. Yet I do so because most of us know so little about the Lord's Prayer.

Lord, Teach Us to Pray

1

The Lord's Prayer in the Bible and Today

The Lord's Prayer in the Bible

In the Bible, we find two versions of the Lord's Prayer, one in Matthew and the other in Luke. The Matthew version (set in the Sermon on the Mount) is longer.

Pray then like this:

Our Father who art in heaven,
Hallowed be thy name.
Thy kingdom come.
Thy will be done,
On earth as it is in heaven.
Give us this day our daily bread;

He was praying in a certain place,
and when he ceased,
one of his disciples said to him,
"Lord, teach us to pray,
as John taught his disciples."
And he said to them,
"When you pray, say:
"Father,
hallowed be thy name.
Thy kingdom come.
Give us each day our daily bread;

And forgive us our debts,
As we also have forgiven our
debtors;

And lead us not into
temptation,
But deliver us from evil.
(Matt. 6:9-13, RSV)

and forgive us our sins,
for we ourselves forgive every
one who is indebted to
us;
and lead us not into
temptation."

(Luke 11:1-4, RSV)

Of course, the source of the different versions is debated by scholars. Some believe Jesus said this prayer only once and his disciples and other editors subsequently recorded what they remembered, possibly amending it later on. Chronologically, Matthew and Luke give a different place to the Lord's Prayer. Its placement and arrangement may be solely the result of editing.

I suspect Jesus found many occasions to teach *versions* of the Lord's Prayer. If so, the fact that he used different words shows that the specific words recorded may not be that important. We might have room to vary the vocabulary.

In the 1930s, C. K. Ogden simplified English into an 850 word system known as "Basic" (British American Scientific International Commercial). In Basic, the Lord's Prayer is translated,

> Father of all up in the sky,
> You get our deepest respect.
> We hope your nation with you as king for ruler
> will come down to us.
> We hope you have your way
> in the place we live as on high.
> Give us food for now,
> and overlook wrongdoing
> as we overlook wrongdoing by persons to us.
> Please guide us from courses of desire,
> and keep us from badness.

Intriguingly, the Lord's Prayer as we recite it in our churches and rituals is *not* in our Bibles. No accurate translation of the Lord's Prayer includes the word *trespass*, but that word is found in the familiar liturgical forms of this prayer. Similarly, there is no doxology in the Bible's version of the Lord's Prayer. The main significance of the prayer is not its specific words but what it teaches us about prayer and about our relationship to God.

Biblical scholars are often helpful but can confuse us if we take them too seriously. Thus, for example, when they analyze the Lord's Prayer, all offer different interpretations of its divisions.

Some divide the prayer in two main parts. The first three petitions (hallowed be thy name, thy kingdom come, thy will be done) are about God. The last four (give us this day our daily bread, forgive us our debts, lead us not into temptation, deliver us from evil) are about humans.

Others also divide the prayer in two parts but say the first four petitions (hallowed be thy name, thy kingdom come, thy will be done, give us this day our daily bread) ask God for good things. The last three ask God to help us avoid evil (forgive us our debts, lead us not into temptation, deliver us from evil).

Still others see a threefold division. The first three petitions are for God's welfare (hallowed be thy name, thy kingdom come, thy will be done). The fourth request is for our physical welfare (give us this day our daily bread). The last three are petitions for our spiritual welfare (forgive us our debts, lead us not into temptation, deliver us from evil).

This shows that, in matters of prayer, one cannot easily separate the concerns of God from the welfare of humans, worship of God from love of neighbor, or desire for spiritual blessings from petitions for human well-being. In prayer, all is connected.

Leonardo Boff analyzes the prayer this way.

> The first part speaks on God's behalf: the Father, keeping his name holy, his kingdom, his holy will. The second part is concerned with human interests: our daily bread, forgiveness, ever-present temptation, and ever-threatening evil.
>
> . . . God is not just interested in what belongs to him: his name, his kingdom, his divine will. He is also concerned about our affairs: bread, forgiveness, temptation, evil. Likewise we are not just concerned with what is vital to us: bread, forgiveness, temptation, evil. We are also open to the Father's concerns: sanctification of God's name, the coming of God's kingdom, the realization of God's will."[1]

There are differences between Matthew's and Luke's presentations of the Lord's Prayer. But both introduce this prayer in a larger context of *teaching* on prayer. In Matthew, Jesus presents this longer version of the prayer while teaching about prayer. In Luke, the disciples see Jesus praying and ask him for help. This is the *only* prayer Jesus actually teaches in all of the gospels.

Today there is a revival of interest in prayer and spirituality. Secularism has failed to nurture us at the deepest levels of our beings. Unfortunately, much of our quest for true spirituality looks far afield—yet old sources can often nourish us well. The Lord's Prayer is one such reliable source.

I find it helpful to repeat the Lord's Prayer as handed down. It is also important, however, to remember Jesus did not say to "pray this exactly." Jesus simply said to "pray *like* this." In any case, we cannot pray one definitive form of the Lord's Prayer, because we have received different versions of it. Lohmeyer, in the best book available on the Lord's Prayer, says that "it speaks of the way to pray, not of these particular words of prayer."[2]

This prayer, like all true prayer, teaches and reminds us of our basic dependence on God. The fact that the disciples asked for help to pray was in itself significant. They realized that their old traditions were no longer nourishing them, even as they had a deep thirst for God. Thus today we too can turn to the Lord's Prayer for help in the nurture of our faith and spirituality.

Through all these many centuries, ever since Jesus taught it, the Lord's Prayer has helped us learn to pray. But this is no easy learning. Paradoxically, though we are familiar with the Lord's Prayer it always has something more to teach us. It can always bear more exploration and reflection, especially since we know the Lord's Prayer so well.

Joachim Jeremias writes that

> just because the Lord's Prayer is profound, we need ever new attempts to fathom its meaning for our day. Because it is familiar, we need to hear its contents restated in a way that can jab our prayers awake. Because it is remote, we face dangers in praying it today. It speaks of a "Father in heaven," and we live in a space age where "heaven" is a dubious concept and [people] have their own ideas about the "father-image." It hopes for "kingdom come," in a day when [people] see only this present materialistic age. In our affluent society this prayer seems to talk simply of "daily bread." It

> seems to seek immunity from temptation in a world where we know everything consists of shades of gray. . . . Precisely because this prayer seems twenty centuries . . . removed from our thought world, we need a guide to lead us through its ancient landmarks, so that we may pray as Jesus first taught and encouraged his disciples to pray.[3]

The Challenge of Praying the Lord's Prayer Today

We are in danger of taking the Lord's Prayer for granted. Yet it needs continual use and exploration. Lohmeyer writes that "the Lord's Prayer offers an inexhaustible content, which can always be grasped and repeated by the prayer of heart and mouth, yet never fathomed in the thoughts of the mind."[4]

Some of us lobby for use of the Lord's Prayer in public schools. But in the early church, only full members had access to the Lord's Prayer, just as only full members could participate in the Lord's Supper. Only those baptized were taught the Lord's Prayer. Being permitted to pray the Lord's Prayer was a serious and privileged responsibility.

In those days the Lord's Prayer was treated with reverence and awe. Some Christian traditions still show that reverential attitude. In certain liturgical traditions, people only pray the Lord's Prayer *after* the priest first prays, "And make us *worthy*, O Lord, that we joyously and without presumption may make bold to invoke Thee, the heavenly God as Father, and to say: Our Father. . . ."

In those early days of the church, the Lord's Prayer was not repeated publicly by the entire worshiping congregation. Rather it was a secret as taught to believers as they were prepared for baptism. "The prayer therefore became a mark of . . . new commitment to the Christian faith and the Christian community."[5]

There were several reasons for this. This prayer was regarded as too holy for people not properly trained, prepared, and taught. And the prayer was too radical and subversive. In a Roman culture that venerated and worshiped Caesar, it was literally treason to pray the Lord's Prayer—"allegiance to the empire was determined by proclaiming the kingship of the emperors, the holiness of their name. . . . To declare otherwise, as demanded by [this prayer] was to act subversively."[6] The Lord's Prayer was too dangerous to be used in public.

But now the Lord's Prayer has been cheapened into the very vain petition Jesus warned against. Cheapened because routinely repeated without being meant or heard. Perverted because often an empty and meaningless ritual. Distorted when used by Caesar or the government in whatever ceremonies. Torn from its roots and rendered meaningless when taught as a rote learning in state-funded schools.

I do not believe the Lord's Prayer should be taught in public schools. This only distorts the intent of the prayer and uses the gospel for ways in which it was not intended. I agree with Gene L. Davenport, who says that "disciples must reject any effort to make the prayer a part of secular activities, such as public school classrooms, which . . . are gathering places of the world under the dominion of Caesar."[7]

I have heard many arguments for the Lord's Prayer in school. Some claim the prayer has a good calming effect on children. But surely we can find better ways to still the restlessness of children. We do not advocate state-sponsored baptisms in the washroom for cleaning dirty children or state-sponsored communions in the cafeteria to still hungry stomachs. Likewise I cannot support using the Lord's Prayer as a pedagogical technique to manipulate children into being peaceful.

We no longer feel much reverence before the Lord's Prayer. Jeremias writes that if Matthew or Luke experienced "our use of the Lord's Prayer in a mixed group of Christians, or our habit of 'repeating together the Lord's Prayer' as a convenient device to close any . . . meeting, might he not be shocked that we have moved so far from its original use?"[8]

Some authors criticize other repetitions of the Lord's Prayer too. When I was seventeen, a musical version of the Lord's Prayer (sung by an Australian nun) made the musical charts. This folksy version was sung on rock and roll radio stations. Some of my friends pondered whether this version of the Lord's Prayer violated Jesus' command against vain repetition. If they had looked in their hymnals, they would have found many other musical versions of the Lord's Prayer.

More telling criticisms of this modern musical phenomenon came from Michael Crosby. He wonders how Christians have come to use the prayer to make money and asks, "How can we get excited about hearing the Lord's Prayer played over the airwaves sandwiched between a sexist remark by a chauvinist male disc jockey and an ad for Preparation H?"[9]

While we may be too casual in repeating the Lord's Prayer, I do believe that it bears repeating, as do any great hymns, prayers, and ordinances. All repetitions are not automatically vain. When a congregation prays the Lord's Prayer, it becomes a focus of united prayer. As long as this is not mindless repetition, the prayer unites us not only with God and his kingdom, and not only with each other—but also with all Christians elsewhere.

Our unity with others in God's kingdom is a key aspect of this prayer. The Lord's Prayer—indeed all true prayer—is never for our benefit alone. William Barclay notes the community thrust of prayer from an ancient Jewish prayer. " 'Let not the prayer of wayfarers find entrance, O Lord, before thee.' The idea is that the wayfarer might be asking for fine weather when the country as a whole needed rain."[10] Barclay then notes that the Lord's Prayer speaks of our and us, but never of I, me, my, and mine.

Thus as we pray the Lord's Prayer, we can expect to be afflicted and confronted and made uncomfortable. This prayer does not promise us security, wealth or prosperity.

Lord, Teach Us to Pray

Parents often tell their children, "I love you." Sometimes I say it so often that my kids get exasperated with me. "I know, I know," they respond.

Of course, our children also mimic us and repeat our words. "I love you," they say. Although they use the same words as adults, they do not mean the same thing as adults. They do not even fully understand the meaning of their words.

When an adult tells a child, "I love you," the emotional meaning and depth of the phrase is deep and complex. A mother might be thinking about having carried the child in her womb for nine months and the incredible physical bonds that link mother and child. A father might remember his anxiety as he watched his wife's body change and wondered about the new life forming within.

When a parent says, "I love you," the parent knows there is no other child in the world special in quite that way. No other child, no other voice makes one's heart stop. When a parent says, "I love you," he or she remembers the sense of gratefulness to God for such a precious gift.

A parent knows how much the child's arrival has changed his or her life. A parent remembers the first tooth, the first word, the first step. A parent remembers the worry and hard work, the anxiety over an illness or an injury, and the exhaustion of non-stop caretaking. And a parent makes a commitment to love the child, no matter what, for the child's whole life.

As I tell my children I love them, I also come to understand more and more what it means to have my parents love me. I find myself increasingly appreciating and loving my parents. Thus the meaning of saying "I love you" becomes deeper and richer all the time.

The "I love you" of children is simpler. In part, children just repeat the words without really understanding them. In part, they know those words are expected. Children are less conscious of connectedness to a parent.

But they do know that no one is as pretty or handsome as their parents. No voice sounds as nice as a parent's. No one else can make the ouchies go away with just a kiss. No one else fits just right in a hug. Children say, "I love you," and know there is something different and special about their parents, something that cannot be matched or replaced by anyone else.

When we teach our children to say, "I love you," we cannot expect them to *understand* what they say. Yet it is not wrong to teach them the words. The words are true, even when not understood.

All my life I told my parents I loved them. It was always true, even though it becomes an increasingly complex reality. It was true when I was an accepting child. It was true when I was a rebellious adolescent. It is still true (only more so) now that I am an adult and myself a parent.

They are words that are always true and words that we can always grow into. As the years go by, we understand them better and better. As parents, we are in the best position to give to our children the words they need in our relationship.

When I was a youth, I found it easy to pray. In the evenings, I used to go out to the field behind our house and speak with God at great length. I could talk to him for an hour at a time.

But as the years went by, I found it harder and harder to pray. Part of it grew from my anguish over the death of my sister. Sometimes I no longer knew what to talk about with God. Part of it came from doubts about prayer—if God already knew everything, what should I tell him?

I can easily relate to the sentiments of one writer.

> I suspect that our failed attempts to pray more often lie partly in this dread of not knowing what to say, in our ambivalence about sitting still in God's presence, unprotected by distraction, unhidden by the facile words that seem to get us by in everyday speech. Like the writer's proverbial blank page waiting to be filled with prose, the prospect of addressing God can intimidate us into silence.[11]

There was a time in my life when I was completely stymied and did not know how to pray.

But eventually I learned to pray again. I did it by praying the prayers handed down through the Bible and the church. Thus I value the Lord's Prayer and the Psalms. I pray with them. Sometimes I do not understand what I am praying. Sometimes I am unable to pray. But in submitting to the discipline of the handed-down prayers, I find myself praying even when thinking I cannot pray. The given prayers are much like the love formula taught to us by our parents.

The Lord's Prayer is a gift. Its words help us when we are immature in our faith, and they are words that we can always grow into. Martin Luther said: "To this day I am still nursing myself on the Lord's Prayer like a child and am still eating and drinking of it like an old man without getting bored with it."[12] As our Father and Creator, God is in the best position to give us the words that we need in our relationship with him.

Even so, Lord, teach us to pray.

2

Our Father

> "Our Father" (Matthew: RSV, NRSV, NIV, NEB, NAB, JB)
> "Father" (Luke: RSV, NRSV, NIV, NEB, NAB, JB)

The Importance of "Our"

The very first word in Matthew's version of the Lord's Prayer, *our*, can inspire much discussion and reflection. It immediately reminds us of the corporate nature of this important Christian prayer—and all Christian prayer.

The Heidelberg Catechism calls this prayer "Our Lord's Prayer." This is a somewhat confusing title. In Detroit, near the Windsor-Detroit tunnel, is a church sign that reads "Old Mariners' Church." I never know whether this is the older edition of the Mariners' Church (and the newer church building is elsewhere) or whether this means this is a church for old Mariners.

Likewise, I do not know whether the Heidelberg Catechism's title means that this is the prayer of *our Lord* or this prayer is *ours*—belonging to you and me. Either interpretation is a good one. Protestants generally simply refer to the "Lord's Prayer." Roman Catholics, on the other hand, call it "the *Our* Father" and speak of praying the "Our Father." Note again the importance of the word *our* (although Luke does not use the word at all).

Our is not a popular word these days. We admire rugged individuals and Lone Rangers. I was reminded of this again when my wife and I went on vacation some time ago. On the whole, we have similar standards for judging the merits of vacations. If we can do a lot of quiet, uninterrupted reading, we are happy.

But I do have one standard Lorna does not share. When I found that our hotel had HBO, I was enthusiastic. Lorna was blasé. But she was less than blasé when she saw me watching the movie *Leviathan*. This underwater thriller was billed as a "screamfest." I like thrillers; Lorna doesn't. (A friend of mine, an ordained United Methodist pastor with a doctorate in film, has an impressive theological rationale for watching suspense movies. But I just like them—for no particularly good reason.)

Leviathan is about an underwater mining crew which uncovers a dangerous disease. It consumes the crew one by one, joining and blending them into a horrific sea creature. At a climactic point, one crew member (a doctor) decides that if they escape from the monster by getting to the water's surface, they will expose the world to the threat of this horrible beast.

The doctor concludes that it would be better for the half dozen to die and save the world. In the film, this fellow is seen as deluded, a servant of the beast. Two others manage to overcome the doctor's desires and do escape to the surface. In so doing, they risk exposing the world to Leviathan.

In some societies, the doctor would be a hero. He practiced self-sacrifice for the wider good. But in our culture, the two escapees are heroes. One man and one woman are rugged, self-interested, selfishly heroic, and courageous individuals. They are brave and daring. At the end of the movie, the man slugs a female corporate executive. This monster-slaying woman-basher is the hero of the film.

But I still think the real hero was the martyred doctor. He has more to teach us than the survivors of the terror. For according to the Bible (and re-echoed in the first word of the Lord's Prayer), self-sacrifice is more important than self-interest, community is more vital than status, and fellowship is better than success.

Life brings us many obstacles and leviathans. We seek to conquer our problems and to achieve our hopes. Our culture says we can best do this on our own, by ourselves, without the help of others. We can be most successful and secure as individuals or (at most) a nuclear family.

We face leviathans without and within—of loneliness, insecurity, desolation, unworthiness, guilt, grief, frustration, and hopelessness. In our culture, we can find no solution for these except within our solitary selves. Supposedly the bigger and braver you are, the more able you are to conquer your Leviathans. Our competitive culture tells us to worship the daring, rough, and hardy individuals who can kill Leviathans and slay all other threats.

But the Bible teaches otherwise. We can never be smart, strong, rough, or even good enough to slay all our leviathans. The leviathans that most plague us can only be solved by God, our Father. Thus the Psalmist proclaims to God, "*You* crushed the heads of Leviathan" (Ps. 74:14, emphasis added). And we turn to God and rely on God within the community of faith.

The first word of this prayer, "our," grabs, shakes, and startles us. It reverses many understandings about our relationship to God. Our individualistic society values personal privacy; thus we like to think of God as someone we relate to in complete privacy. But praying to our Father immediately reminds us that in praying to God we ally ourselves with many others—other Christians, other brothers and sisters, other children of our Father in heaven.

The Lord's Prayer, then, is subversive. It undermines many of our society's understandings and creeds. One book on the Lord's Prayer is appropriately subtitled, *Praying the Our Father As Subversive Activity*.[1] This prayer challenges individualism. It was subversive when Jesus first taught it and it remains more so today because it remains radical and new.

Prayer is never just a private, personal, individualistic relationship to God. When we pray, we join with the whole body of Christ. We become part of the cloud of witnesses, the communion of the saints. Even if we pray alone, we are not alone. We may be the only one in our room or even our house, but we are not alone. When we pray, we are part of Christ's body worshiping and praying around the world. We are also part of the communion of saints throughout history.

Unfortunately, in the realm of spirituality, we often think and act individualistically. Henri Nouwen confesses,

> In the intimacy of my relationship with God I still find myself thinking more about my faith, my hope and my love than about our faith, our hope and our love. I worry about *my* individual prayer life, I speculate about *my* future as an educated man, and I reflect on how much good I have done or will do for others. In all of this, it is my individual spiritual life that receives most of the attention.[2]

Prayer may sometimes be private. But it is never only private. It may be personal, but it is never only personal. Praying our Lord's Prayer together is a corporate discipline reminding us that in prayer we are always part of God's larger family. We never *only* relate to God alone. To be fully God's children, God expects us to be part of the church, the body of Christ. God is the Lord over a nation, a kingdom.

I am uncomfortable with talk about "accepting Jesus as my personal Lord and Savior." Jesus is not a *personal* Lord and Savior if by that we mean, as we often do, that Jesus is our *private* Savior. Jesus cannot be a private Lord and Savior. The phrase is a contradiction in terms. No one can individually own God.

Queen Elizabeth is no one's private queen or monarch. George Bush is no one's private president. Brian Mulroney is no one's private prime minister. The very definition of such offices as lord, monarch, queen, president, or prime minister demands a nation. *Queen*, by definition, implies a group, as does *president*, *prime minister*, and *lord*. Following Jesus as our Lord and Savior means that he is not merely our individual Lord.

Jesus is *our* Lord and Savior. Having saved us, he rules over us. Indeed, he is the ruler of the universe and he died for the sins of the world—"and through him God was pleased to reconcile to himself all things, whether on earth or in heaven, by making peace through the blood of his cross" (Col. 1:20).

Jesus does desire our personal allegiance and heartfelt commitment. But such a decision does not make him our private Lord and Savior. It merely means that we have accepted his authority in our lives and joined with the body of people who have similarly accepted his authority.

Certainly I (and each one of us) must personally and individually respond to Jesus' invitation. Each of us is called to account. But what we accept is the *corporate* and *universal* authority of Jesus Christ. We must beware of language that tries to make God's relationship with us too individualistic or private. Similarly, pious language such as "my Jesus, my sweet Jesus" can be deceptive, mistaken, misleading, and even dangerous.

James Houston says that "intimacy [with God] can only be shared, which is why we pray *'Our* Father.' No child of God can live in isolation."[3] Thus the Lord's Prayer is replete with "ours" and "us." Thus, nowhere in our Lord's Prayer do we find the words *I, me, myself, my,* or *mine.*

On Being God's Children

The fracture of Christian community is always a tragedy. I remember visiting a monastery once where I knew the monks to be at war with one another. Conflicts and divisions raged. Then they chanted Psalm 133 together.

> How very good and pleasant it is
>   when kindred live together in unity!
> It is like the precious oil on the head,
>   running down upon the beard,
> on the beard of Aaron,
>   running down over the collar of his robes.
> It is like the dew of Hermon
>   which falls upon the mountains of Zion.
> For there the Lord has ordained his blessing,
>   life forevermore. (Psalm 133)

In that context, the song was filled with haunting pathos. While they were as yet unable to live in unity, I saw it as a prayerful (even pitiful) plea for peace. For they knew the importance of praying together.

Individualism is a prevailing myth of our day and age, but it is a myth that our Lord's Prayer undermines and overthrows. Rampant individualism cannot be meshed with biblical spirituality. The gospel shows us that we are not merely or only individuals. Rather, we are bound to each by many bonds.

One year, I escorted Mennonites from the small, rural Ontario town of Leamington to my former neighborhood in Chicago. As I pondered the nature of "Our Father" in Chicago, I became aware of many new connections. I knew I was not just accompanying a group of individual young people. I watched over them carefully and gave them important guidelines, because I was accountable to the wider church community back in Leamington.

I brought my friends to Chicago with the hope that they would realize their connectedness to the wider world. That did happen in beautiful ways. Folks found joy in service and came to a deeper understanding of their bonds to the suffering in Chicago. The pain they saw deeply hurt them.

One of our students struck up a meaningful friendship with a gang kid, Jorge. Eventually, Jorge opened up and told our student much about life in the ghetto. He even showed his bullet scars, much as Jesus once displayed his wounds to Thomas. That emerging relationship in such a short time was a small miracle that pointed to the truth that we are all children of one Father.

When we pray our Lord's Prayer, we remind ourselves that God is Father to many people. In one sense at least God is the Father to all of us, since he created us all.

> Is not he your father, who created you
> who made you and established you?
> (Deut. 32:6b; cf. Isa. 64:8)

Certainly, the Creator calls us to love, care for, and nurture his creation as his representatives on earth.

But there is a deeper meaning to being God's children. Being God's children is not automatically conferred upon us as a right. Although we are all created by God, we are not his natural children. We are God's children as a gift of the Holy Spirit.

> For all who are led by the Spirit of God are children of God. For you did not receive a spirit of slavery to fall back into fear, but you have received a spirit of adoption. When we cry, "Abba! Father!" it is that very Spirit bearing witness with our spirit that we are children of God. (Rom. 8:14-16)

Being God's children is a matter of *adoption,* Paul says. It is an adoption that we must accept. Jesus also made clear that *obedience* is intimately related to being God's child. "Whoever does the will of God is my brother and sister and mother" (Matt. 12:50). "My mother and my brothers are those who hear the word of God and do it" (Luke 8:21).

Accepting God as *our* Father, becoming obedient to him, and recognizing our connectedness to others through God is a great challenge. It also means accepting God's family, accepting those brothers and sisters God gives us—whether we like them or not.

> The designation 'God's children' is not exclusive; it is not intended to lead to pride and snobbery before the world. On the contrary, it is one that indicates responsibility to be about the Father's business of drawing all creatures into his family. The task of the children is to be the Father's instruments in increasing the family until it includes the entire world.[4]

Many writers note that Jesus' Aramaic word for God, *Abba,* implied great intimacy, tenderness, and familiarity, much like our word *Daddy*. Boff marvels at this.

> It . . . never entered into anyone's head to use this familiar, commonplace expression to refer to God. That would be failing to show respect. . . . And yet Jesus, in all his prayers . . . addressed God with the expression "Dearest Father" . . . one hundred seventy times in the Gospels.[5]

While the Old Testament referred to God as "Father" fourteen times, Jesus pushed us into new realms when he called God Abba. No reverent Jew would have dared call God "Father." Yet Jesus almost always did so.

Even more surprising is that Jesus gave *us* permission to call God Abba. Before God, we must be childlike. "Truly I tell you, unless you change and become like children, you will never enter the kingdom of heaven" (Matt. 18:3). Being permitted—even commanded—to call God "Father" is a tremendous privilege which gives us powerful access to God. "And because you are children, God has sent the Spirit of his Son into our hearts, crying, 'Abba! Father!' So you are no longer a slave but a child, and if a child then also an heir, through God" (Gal. 4:6-7).

Hugging God

It is appropriate that this prayer reflects the intimacy between parent and child. When I was a child, my sister and I often posed this question to our parents after supper: "Can I sit on you?" Now I enjoy it when one of my children sits on my lap.

Prayer is a way of hugging God. People need physical contact to be healthy. I occasionally hear statistics about how many hugs per day a person needs. "Two are better than one. . . . Again, if two lie together, they keep warm; but how can one keep warm alone?" (Eccl. 4:9a, 11). One problem with abandoned or premature babies is that the lack of physical touching could cause permanent damage. Thus nurses often make sure to give extra physical attention to babies that are alone or abandoned.

When my children climb into my lap for a hug or just to be held, they do not calculate the benefits or effects. They touch spontaneously and naturally. Somehow they know that being held by a parent soothes, comforts, even helps heal wounds. They come when they feel like it, when they have been injured, when their feelings have been hurt, or when they are afraid.

But my children do not only come for hugs when they feel special needs. We hug each other regularly and frequently. That routine hugging makes the "emergency hugs" all the more effective. Even when we are alone and feeling lonely, the memory of regular hugging can nurture and comfort us.

Parents know healthy relationships require physical touch. Although the effects are not easily measurable, in the long run everyone benefits from good hugs. We can't precisely analyze the costs and benefits of hugs, yet we know they are important.

The same dynamics apply to prayer. Our spiritual health calls for regular contact with God, and God delights to be in touch with us. Prayer transcends calculations about costs and effectiveness. The benefits of prayer are often long-term, even invisible. Yet prayer nurtures our lives, bringing comfort and healing wounds. Thus we may pray to God, not only when in crisis, but as regularly and naturally as a child comes to a parent for a hug. Regular prayer makes our "foxhole prayers" more meaningful.

Abba, can I hug you?

3

Our Father and the Sins of Our Fathers

Do Sinful Fathers Represent God?

In chapter two I claimed that it is a *privilege* to call God "Father." The phrase, "*our* Father" calls us to community and unity, but the very name *Father* scandalizes and divides. One must address the problem of God's *masculine* name. I write hesitantly, as one with predictably male biases. My conclusions contradict those of many people I most esteem.

People have always had difficulty with their fathers. Too many fathers were abusive, dictatorial, and neglectful. Many friends were beaten, abused (emotionally or otherwise), or neglected by their fathers. Kierkegaard's problems with his own father, for example, led to difficulties in relating to God.

Diane Tennis delineates ways fathers fail. These can include being more committed to work than to family, abandoning families and leaving custody to mothers, being emotionally distant, and being dangerous. (Fathers are the major source of child abuse, including most sexual abuse.)[1]

We are uneasy with God as Father because of poor and evil fathers, especially those who justified themselves by claiming to represent God. Rather than evaluating God by human fathers, however, we should measure such humans by how they fall short of God's priorities. Even good fathers fail in significant ways. Although my children are still young, I have already sinned against them more times than I can count.

When we think of sinful fathers, how can we call God our Father?

Jesus knew no male parent could adequately represent God. "Call no one your father on earth, for you have one Father—the one in heaven" (Matt. 23:9). Perhaps we should ask whether we can call any man a true father.

Speaking of God, we use metaphors, images, and parables. All metaphors create problems. It is not enough then to call God "Mother." In our culture women have not had the same power (and therefore not the same opportunities to abuse power) as men, but women and mothers also sin.

Any metaphors cause problems. God is aware of how families fail us. The psalmist writes, "For my father and my mother have forsaken me, but the Lord will take me up" (Ps. 27:10, RSV).

Our Father Versus Our Fathers

A close friend had a neglectfully absent father. "I call God 'Father' since he is *not like* my father. God is better than my father," she says.

God our Father is better than our fathers. Feminism cautions *against* idolizing fathers. Good parents teach by modest parallels. Bad parents teach by contrast. "God as Father is always more than all positive experiences of fathers and measures all negative experiences of fathers by the criterion of God's fatherhood."[2]

Calling God "Father" does not suggest God is like our fathers. Rather, fathers are challenged to higher standards. A feminist writes, "I take no offense at the father God because he . . . stands over against all fathers who lay claim to a godlike authority. A mother God would be the same standard for mothers; but I think that fathers still need it more."[3]

Australian culture has problems with its fathers. There, fathers are "very uninvolved in family life. It is common for the men to work all day and go to the pub all evening. So, children . . . have little perception of what a 'loving father' is."[4] It is important to remind such men of God as Father. Australian and all fathers need the witness of a loving Father as a challenging model. Biblical metaphors of God helped transform an ancient culture.

> Through faith in this God . . . human fathering in the biblical community was gradually transformed. Males . . . became more secure (Prov. 14:26), and hence less needful of heroics in establishing their identities. To walk humbly with their God, and, like him, to care for others became the male cultural ideal (Mic. 6:8). . . . As a consequence, marital fidelity and love were progressively extolled (Prov. 5:18-20; Gen. 2:24; Song 8:6f.; Mal. 2:13-6) and women generally were less feared and more appreciated by men as their "counterparts" or equals. (Gen. 2:18-23)[5]

We need such positive influences, especially as our society becomes more and more fatherless.

> While millions of children are deprived of appropriately caretaking fathers by conditions brought about by the industrial revolution, millions more are virtually being abandoned by fathers caught up in the sexual revolution.[6]

Our Father's name does not automatically lead to male power abuse. (No more than terms such as "King of kings" or "Lord of lords" inevitably leads to "the divine right of kings.") The Bible calls God "Father" to emphasize compassionate tenderness (qualities some consider *maternal*). God models an intimacy that is intended to transform all our human relationships.

Patriarchal Projections?

Some cannot identify with a God described by masculine metaphors. What does it mean for women to be in God's image? Some of my friends lost their faith over this issue. Paradoxically, others grew greatly in faith while struggling with this. As a male, I realize I cannot fully comprehend such pain.

Some alter the Lord's Prayer to "Our Father-Mother," "Our Mother," "Our Father and Mother." In Evanston, Illinois, the Wheadon United Methodist congregation rewrote the Lord's Prayer.

> Our God,
> who art with us
> and beyond us,
> hallowed be thy name.
> Thy new earth come,
> thy will be done,
> on earth as it is in promise.
> Give us this day our daily bread.
> And forgive us our sin
> as we forgive those who sin against us.
> And lead us not into temptation,
> but deliver us from evil.
> For thine is the new earth
> and the power
> and the glory
> forever. . . .
>
> (The word "*king*dom" is also deleted; it too has gender implications.)

Some argue that language describing God is a patriarchal projection of sexist culture. Jesus could not call God "Mother" in his culture. That awaited a more enlightened age. One author complains that the NRSV Bible translation did not use inclusive language for God. "The language of males, applied to God, is merely a metaphor. But it also reflects the patriarchal power structure of those who use that metaphor."[7] That writer argues that translators should change the way the Bible refers to God because the original male biblical editors could or would not. In many churches, no reference is made to the Trinity of "Father, Son, and Holy Ghost." Rather, people praise "Creator, Redeemer, and Sustainer."

Some new descriptions of God get away from understanding God in relational terms. They cease addressing *who* God is and settle for *what* God does. God is related to as a *function*, not a person. God becomes not Father but Creator; not Son but Redeemer; not Holy Spirit but Sustainer. For years, a feminist friend addressed God neutrally as "God." Over time, she felt God's personhood eroded. She lost a sense of relationship with God.

Retaining the "Father"

It *was* an option in biblical times to address God as female. Most surrounding religions had masculine and feminine principles represented among their gods.[8] Some matriarchal societies and goddess religions oppressed women. Female god-names do not guarantee liberation.

Israelite faith was virtually the only religion to represent one god. And it did so solely in masculine terms. In most of his prayers, Jesus addressed God as "Father." Some believe that the (male) interpreters of revelation were culturally-limited. This is possible—but not certain.

"Father" is not about maleness but about *relationship*. It is about a relationship that is loving, intimate—and also transcendent. Metaphors for God do not prove men are superior, justify patriarchal social structures, or show that male experience is superior.

Male God-metaphors can indeed be used to exploit women. Some argue that women must not be ordained, because they cannot represent Christ. But gender does not affect representing Christ. Male-dominated God-language should not be used to oppress women, as "there is no longer male and female; for all of you are one in Christ Jesus" (Gal. 3:28).

God's experience also reflects women's experiences. Biblical metaphors show God's experiences as a birth-giver, nursing mother, midwife, homemaker.[9] Yet the Bible never alludes to God as female.

> His love is compared to that of a mother and his work to that of women in labor; . . . his Father-hood is maternal in its caring tenderness. Yet . . . the Bible addresses him in masculine terminology, making amply clear that such terms go far beyond human fatherhood. . . . God is "holy," . . . totally other than anything or anyone one in all creation, far beyond the created differentiation of sexuality. His transcendence breaks every metaphor that would limit his qualitative otherness.[10]

Biblical traditions best reflect God's intentions by reinforcing the dignity of *both* women and men, working for their reconciliation. In the gospels, Jesus calls God "Father" 170 times. Some argue that Jesus deliberately and self-consciously used "Father" as a way of breaking the sexist power of patriarchy! Elizabeth Schussler Fiorenza notes that "Jesus uses the 'father' name of God not as a legitimization for existing patriarchal power structures in church or society but as a critical subversion of all structures of domination."[11]

Willard M. Swartley notes that "where the New Testament portrays God as Father, a woman's . . . roles are very positive. . . . Conversely, where women's roles are restricted by interconnection to patriarchal structures (1 Cor. 14:34-35; 1 Tim. 2:11-12), God is not portrayed as Father."[12] Biblical gender language unsettles *everyone*. Old Testament descriptions of God's fatherhood imply both authority *and* motherly tenderness.[13] The tender "Abba" also shows God's mercy and closeness.[14]

Eugene Peterson's high view of the Book of Revelation can be applied to the whole Bible. Revelation reminds us

> that scripture is God's word to us, not human words about God. Reading scripture as if it were the writings of various persons throughout history giving their ideas or experiences of God, is perhaps the commonest mistake that is made in reading scripture. And the deadliest.[15]

The Scriptures are not merely culturally-determined, penned by chauvinists, blindered by patriarchal limitations. They are not just for teaching, study, and analysis. They are for prayer, meditation on God's priorities, and worship. They are meant to be prayed with the heart.

I pray the Psalms, for example, and they help me grow, even as I have trouble with some Psalms. The violent curses bother me. As a pacifist I have difficulty addressing God with the military title "lord of hosts."

Praying the Psalms goes beyond politically-motivated analysis. "These are not words that we laboriously but impersonally study, as if for an exam. . . . These are words we *take* in—words designed for shaping new life in us."[16] I dare not censor or rewrite Psalms or other God-given prayers that unsettle me. I pray the Psalms as they are handed down.

Some will accuse me of bibliolatry, making an idol of the Bible.

But my intent is simply to see the Bible as a unique source of revelation. We are uniquely able to worship God *through* the Bible's words.

Praying the Lord's Prayer as handed down to us in Scripture helps us approach God and can nourish us.

> If we censor texts or alter them, so that they uniformly say what we want them to say, then we have merely made the texts speak with our own voice. . . . There is no possibility for the Other to reach us in the texts and challenge us to growth and change, because the texts themselves are in no fashion other—they are simply our own voice in a different medium.[17]

Naming and Worship

I once always referred to God as female. In my Master's thesis, I explained,

> God identifies with downtrodden and oppressed persons, thus to call God "he"—identifying her with the traditional oppressors—is . . . problematic. Since God's identification is . . . on the side of the devalued, we finally recognize her to be a "her."

Now I am no longer so ready to discard what is handed down.

We are uneasy with God's masculine metaphors. Just as some pacifists are ill at ease with the portrayals of God as a warrior, many would rather do without the Old Testament (including the Psalms) and Revelation because they violate nonviolent sensibilities. Such well-intentioned notions are misled. God supersedes ideologies and "isms."

We do not worship a sanitized projection of our ideologies, a God fashioned in our image. Any metaphor is limited, "a treasure in earthen vessels" (2 Cor. 4:7, RSV). We dare not throw out the treasure with the vessel. God still communicates truths through limited metaphors.

We do not have to like the metaphors. It is a modern fallacy that we need to feel comfortable with God. The Bible tells us, "It is a fearful thing to fall into the hands of the living God" (Heb. 10:31).

An acquaintance says, "If God is male, then I want to go to

hell!" Dare we impose political (or gender) correctness on God? Dare I say that if God is not Mennonite, then I reject God? Dare I say that if God is not pacifist, then I reject God? Dare I say that if God is not democratic, then I reject God? Yet in these spheres (and others), I am uneasy before God.

Parental Metaphors

My shift from talking about God as feminine to the more traditional metaphors may be a function of getting older and more traditional. Subjectively, my intuition tells me to call God "Father." I thus also must take seriously those whose intuition tell them something else.

My spirituality is influenced by being a parent. When my daughter began talking, she called me "Dada." Yet the name is foreign to me, not fond or familiar. A child of immigrants, I grew up calling my father "Papa." I did not see myself as "Daddy." As her parent, I had the prerogative of naming myself. We patiently taught her to say "Papa," even though I know it sounds foreign in our culture.

When I grew up, I called my father "Pa" instead. When my children grow up, they may change my title to "Pa" or even "Dad." That is part of a maturely developing relationship. However, before God we are always children and God names God.

While there is much that remains unanswered, we dare not abandon the Lord's Prayer's wise teaching that one of God's good names is "Father."

> Do not abandon God the Father, because God as Father is a reliable male symbol in the lives of women and men. Holding on to that reliable Father God can be a way of informing and challenging the status quo. For human fathers are experienced as unreliable. . . . By contrast, God as Father does not abandon. If God the Father is reliable, surely he expects reliability from fathers. And so can we! A reliable Father God is a source of calling men into fathering. A reliable Father God is a source of judgment on unreliable sexual arrangements, a source of hope for women and the fatherless.[18]

4

Providence and Obedience

Our Father Provides

In chapter three, we paid considerable attention to the limits and liabilities of calling God "Father." This name is one of the most important names of God revealed by God. We need to understand what the name suggests.

In chapter two, we saw that "Father" implies a relationship in which we are, like children, adopted. This also makes us related, by adoption, to many other people. Because we are God's children, we are not merely isolated individuals. We are part of a people, a family, a church, and a body.

> Once you were *not a people,*
> but now you *are God's people.* (1 Pet. 2:10)

God's promise to adopt us as his children assures us of his commitments to us. He commits himself to provide for our essential needs. In the Lord's Prayer, Jesus reminds us to pray to God for daily bread, forgiveness of sins, and deliverance from evil and temptation.

Jesus often noted that our heavenly Father intends to supply our basic needs, including material wants. (Later, as we consider the petition "give us this day our daily bread," we will also see this as a call to sharing.) Thus in the Sermon on the Mount, he counsels against anxiety about material things. "For it is the Gentiles who strive for all these things; and indeed your heavenly Father knows that you need all these things" (Matt. 6:32).

We are realizing that busyness and anxiety hinder prayer. In affluent North America, where we could have much time on our hands (since many of us need not worry about survival), we are not people of prayer. I myself am often too busy and anxious to pray. And when I do take time to pray, my busy life does not allow my mind to calm down enough to pray.

> Better is a handful with quiet
> than two handfuls with toil,
> and a chasing after wind. (Eccl. 4:6)

Henri Nouwen warns that busyness and worry hinder our prayers.

> To be preoccupied means to fill our time and place long before we are there. . . . We say to ourselves, "What if I get the flu? What if I lose my job? What if my child is not home on time? What if there is not enough food tomorrow? What if I am attacked? What if a war starts? What if the world comes to an end? What if . . . ?" Much . . . of our suffering is connected with these preoccupations. . . . They prevent us from feeling a real inner freedom. . . .
>
> Our occupations and preoccupations fill our external and internal lives to the brim. They prevent the Spirit of God from breathing freely in us and thus renewing our lives.[1]

It is my and my wife's duty to meet our children's needs. We guarantee them certain provisions. They do not need to plan, to worry, to be anxious. To the best of our ability, we feed, clothe, shelter, protect, and teach them. They mostly have no idea of their needs or how they are met. And so it should be.

> Is there anyone among you who, if your child asks for bread, will give a stone? Or if the child asks for a fish, will give a snake? If you then, who are evil, know how to give good gifts to your children, how much more will your Father in heaven give good things to those who ask him! (Matt. 7:9-11)

We try to raise our children with some basic manners. But we give them what they need whether or not they are polite. We hope they will receive clothes, shelter, food, and teaching with courtesy. But we deliver regardless of our children's behavior.

I often pray for my children, my heart welling up with emotion and concern. I boast to others (those who will listen) of how special and unique my children are. One role of parents is to love their children as no one else does or can, to see the gifts others cannot. God likewise sees each of us as his unique child. God takes precisely such joy in our gifts and individuality.

We stubbornly resist being children before God. We wish to dictate the terms of our relationship. Yet (though human children grow into mature adults) before God we will always be children who must learn obedience and humility.

> When I look at your heavens,
> the work of your fingers,
> the moon and the stars that
> you have established;
> what are human beings that you
> are mindful of them,
> mortals that you care for
> them? (Ps. 8:3-4)

The psalmist, on considering the magnificence of creation and the smallness of humanity, was moved to praise and reverence. The Lord's Prayer moves us similarly. It takes us from a rhythm of magnificent declarations and hopes (hallowed be thy name, thy kingdom come, thy will be done) to preoccupation with earthly concerns (give us this day our daily bread, forgive us our sins, deliver us from evil).

When we contemplate God as our Father, Jesus intends that we be moved to deeper prayer. The Heidelberg Catechism teaches that the purpose of the "our Father" invocation is

> [t]hat at the very beginning of our prayer he may awaken in us the childlike reverence and trust toward God which should be the motivation of our prayer, which is that God has become our Father through Christ and will much less deny us what we ask him in faith than our human fathers will refuse us earthly things.[2]

Doing the Will of Our Father

Elizabeth McAlister likes the idea of God's family so much that she emphasizes it more than God's kingdom. In fact, she talks about the *'kin'*-dom of God rather than the *king*dom of God.[3]

We already saw that the ones adopted into God's family (through the grace of the Holy Spirit) are those who do God's will (Matt. 12:50). Those who obey God the heavenly Father are his children. "Not everyone who says to me, 'Lord, Lord,' will enter the kingdom of heaven, but only the one who does the will of my Father in heaven" (Matt. 7:21).

Obedience to God affects our whole lives and is our highest loyalty. This relationship to God is more important than all other relationships, demands, priorities, or loyalties. "And everyone who has left houses or brothers or sisters or father and or mother or children or fields, for my name's sake, will receive a hundredfold, and will inherit eternal life" (Matt. 19:29). "And call no one your father on earth, for you have one Father—the one in heaven" (Matt. 23:9). "Whoever loves father or mother more than me is not worthy of me; and whoever loves son or daughter more than me is not worthy of me" (Matt. 10:37).

That is why Jesus rebukes a man who makes what we would consider a reasonable request in response to Jesus' call. "Lord, first let me go and bury my father" (Matt. 8:21). That is why the sons of Zebedee are commended as good examples for us. When Jesus called them, "Immediately they left the boat and their *father,* and followed him" (Matt. 4:22).

Our relationship to God the Father is nourished through Jesus the Son. "All things have been handed over to me by my Father; and no one knows the Son except the Father, and no one knows the Father except the Son and anyone to whom the Son chooses to reveal him" (Matt. 11:27). Intimacy with God the Father through Jesus the Son is deepened through prayer.

But such intimacy with God does not make us self-righteous and haughty. Rather, it draws us into deeper concern for the world. To be loved by God as a child transforms us into people who love others and desire to have them join us in God's family.

Our knowledge and love of God results in imitation of God. Our spirituality deepens our resemblance to God, in whose image we are made. "Be perfect, therefore, as your heavenly Father is perfect" (Matt. 5:48). Our good works reflect God the Father himself (Luke 6:36). Those who love their enemies are "children of your Father in heaven" (Matt. 5:45). Those who feed the hungry, welcome the stranger, clothe the naked, care for the sick, and visit the prisoner are welcomed and "blessed by my Father" (Matt. 25:34).

God made us in his image. That image takes shape in us through obedience. Thus our spirituality is fleshed out through good works. "In the same way, let your light shine before others, so that they may see your good works and give glory to your Father in heaven" (Matt. 5:16).

The demands of God are not meant to inspire guilt and feelings of insufficiency. To be like God is an invitation, an opportunity. In George MacDonald's book, *The Maiden's Bequest,* a timid orphan is terrified by a fire and brimstone preacher. She visits her pastor and bursts into tears. Pastor Cowie is disturbed.

> He . . . said with soothing tenderness: "What's the matter . . .?"
>
> After some vain attempts at speech, Annie succeeded in giving the following account of the matter, much interrupted with sobs and fresh outbursts of weeping.
>
> "You see, sir, I went last night to the Missionary kirk to hear Mr. Brown. And he preached a grand sermon. But I haven't been able to bide myself since then. For I'm one of the wicked that God hates, and I'll never get to heaven, for I can't help forgetting Him sometimes. And the wicked'll be turned into hell and all the nations that forget God. And I can't stand it."
>
> In the heart of the good man rose a gentle indignation against the overly pious who had thus terrified and bewildered that precious being, a small child. He thought for a moment.
>
> "You haven't forgotten your father, have you, Annie?" he began.
>
> "I think about him most every day," she answered.
>
> "But there comes a day now and then when you don't think much about him, doesn't there?"
>
> "Yes, sir."
>
> "Do you think he would be angry with his child because she was so much taken up with her books or her play? . . . Do you think he would be angry that you didn't think about him that day, especially when you can't see him?"
>
> "Indeed no, sir. He wouldn't be so sore upon me as that."

"What do you think he would say?"

"If Mr. Bruce were to get after me for it, my father would say: 'Let the lassie alone. She'll think about me another day—there's time enough.' "

"Well, don't you think your Father in heaven would say the same?"

"Maybe He might, sir. But, you see, my father was my own father, and would make the best of me."

"And is not God kinder than your father?" the pastor asked.[4]

Our Response to Fatherly Love

Our actions are never more than responses to God's gracious initiatives. Our actions never match his, never repay his, never equal his. In fact, even as we respond, God continues to make initiatives on our behalf (Matt. 6:26, 7:11, 10:29, 18:10,14). "Alongside the Father who commands and promises, we have in other sayings the Father who cares and loves"[5] God does not ignore or neglect us; he works on our behalf. He

> . . . is the Father who acts for us. Unlike the absentee fathers we may have known, God is present with his people and works to save them. . . . He brought his people out of slavery in Egypt. And in the New Testament he sent his only Son to save us from slavery to sin and to ourselves.[6]

History is replete with absent and abusive fathers. Some human fathers, however, do illustrate the self-giving, sacrificial providence of God. I remember reading of a father who escaped a burning house only to realize his little boy was missing. At the cost of his life, the father reentered the inferno to save the boy.

I once read a novel about a family whose small plane ran out of gas because of headwinds. The plane crashed into the Gulf of Mexico. The family had only one life preserver. Although the parents could have swum to shore, they kept their children floating for two days. But the parents and two of the children eventually succumbed to the waves. Only the smallest lived. His father had secured him to the life preserver and had wrapped a shirt around the boy's head to protect him from the sun.[7] Such is also the love of our Father for us, his children.

5

The Lord Looks Down from Heaven

"Our Father *in heaven*" (Matthew, NRSV, NIV, NEB, NAB, JB)

Close Yet So Far

Mysteriously, our Lord's Prayer moves us immediately from the intimate immanence of God our *Father* to a recognition of God in *heaven*. Heaven is not a popular notion today. In fact, in chapter 2 we saw a modern rewrite of the Lord's Prayer which entirely omits the word: "who art with us and beyond us." Yet the old-fashioned notion of heaven is still relevant.

God resides in heaven, but we look for signs of him here on earth. Douglas V. Steere, the Quaker mystic, visited the world famous cathedral of Chartres, an architectural and devotional masterpiece. His attention was drawn by a figure carved high in an arch.

> In this stone statue God, the Father, holds Adam ever so tenderly on his lap. Adam, however, is asleep with his chin on his chest and his legs and arms drawn up close to his body, almost like a fetus. God is looking at him with deep caring and compassion, as though he longed for his grace to waken Adam . . . [and make him] aware

> of the One whose arms upheld him, and of how much he was being loved. Bernard of Clairvaux's words return at the sight of this picture: God 'loves both more than you and before you love at all.'[1]

Our Lord's Prayer teaches us about the caring and loving parental God who holds us in his lap and loves us without end. That image is true, but believing that alone is incomplete. The opening phrase, "our Father who art in heaven," must be taken as a whole.

In letters, we begin with the address of the recipient and then salute them: "Dear So-and-So." Our Lord's Prayer also opens with an invocation that shows whom we address. Only after uttering this confession do we pray-ers petition God. But we are not just giving an address complete with street and postal code. Our invocation is in itself a confession of whom we believe in. Only after this confession, does the pray-er begin to make petitions.

It is not enough to confess God as Father. A common synagogue prayer invokes "Our Father, Our King." Both truths are held together. Heaven is connected to God's kingship. When Matthew talks about God's kingdom, God's reign, he calls it the "kingdom of *heaven*," where God's perfect will is done.

> The Lord looks down from heaven;
> he sees all humankind.
> From where he sits enthroned he watches
> all the inhabitants of the earth. . . .
> Truly the eye of the Lord is on those who fear him,
> on those who hope in his steadfast love,
> to deliver their soul from death,
> and to keep them alive in famine. (Ps. 33:13-14, 18-19)

The Need for Parental Distance

A good parent is close and intimate, supportive and caring. But a good parent also understands when to stand aside. Parents need to discern when to be present and when to be absent, when to hold on and when to let go, when to attend and when to disregard.

When Lorna and I had only one child, we doted on her. Her smallest stumble sent us into a panic. But now with two children we have neither time nor energy to deal with every child-sized crisis. More and more we count on them to learn to cope for themselves. That too is part of parenting.

Steere tells of another visit to a European cathedral, this time in the Netherlands.

> There is a church . . . that can be reached by climbing up a large, concrete stairway of perhaps one hundred steps. . . . A little three-year-old boy was . . . climbing them all alone one step at a time. His parents were sitting in a little park . . . watching him make his climb. When he got to the top, he stood up in triumph and waved to them. And they beckoned him to begin to make his descent. He soon began to . . . scream for them to come and get him. They sat quietly below and simply beckoned. After . . . a tantrum of anger for their not coming to rescue him, he finally put one foot on the step below, and then another and another. . . . When he got to the bottom, he ran, and they received him into their arms.[2]

Steere observes that this illustrates God's parental relationship with us.

> As I recall this scene, it seemed to give me a clue to the way God has withdrawn in order to give us freedom, even at the risk of our being able to injure ourselves. But God is as deeply involved in this freedom as those wise parents were in their treatment of the child.[3]

This paradox is highlighted by the phrase "our Father who art in heaven." God is as close as a loving parent. But he is also far away in heaven. While he is near, we can only reach him by his initiatives. Theologians use big words here: *immanence* (God's close presence, "our Father") and *transcendence* (God's distant inaccessibility, "who art in heaven"). (While the phrase is not found in Luke's version, it is an important theological assertion.)

Our Lord's Prayer moves quickly from close intimacy to frightening distance. "Am I a God near by, says the Lord, and not a God far off? Who can hide in secret places so that I cannot see them? says the Lord. Do I not fill heaven and earth? says the Lord" (Jer. 23:23-24).

> Christianity is not content with finding God in His immanence . . . it also seeks Him in His infinite transcendence. . . . No system of asceticism, no mystical cult, however esoteric, however pure, can suffice to bridge the abyss between us and this Transcendent Creator of all being. And yet He is our Creator and our Father, and we can speak to Him and hear Him answer us. How? Because He has revealed Himself to us in our own language and has given us human words in which to praise and pray to Him. More than that, He descends into our sphere and takes part in our own life.[4]

Many want only a buddy-buddy god, one we can be friendly with on our own terms. Might the current rebellion against the name "Father" be in part natural human resistance to accepting God on terms that make us uncomfortable? In the Old Testament, people were the opposite—they feared that if they saw God they would die. They feared the idea of a God who would be too near. While God relates to us on familiar and even intimate levels, there are other levels we must acknowledge for the sake of our own spiritual well-being.

> O Lord, our Sovereign,
> how majestic is your name in all the earth! (Ps. 8:1)

Leonardo Boff notes that the phrase "in heaven" symbolizes "the infinite that humankind cannot attain by its own efforts."[5] These mysteries are beyond our words or conceptions. "As creatures of the dust, we are invited into fellowship with the transcendent God who, at the same time, is both as near to us as our breath and as distant as the outer reaches of the cosmos," writes Gene L. Davenport.[6]

Prayer is a doorway to distant heaven. It is the way the heavenly Father permits us to reach him. But it is a risky route, because prayer might allow this transcendent God to take over our lives and shape them according to his will, "on earth as it is in heaven." Prayer does not give us control over the heavenly Father. Through prayer, we begin to realize that the "kingdom of heaven is at hand" (Matt. 10:7, RSV).

The Discipline and the Distance

Because God is distant and transcendent as well as near and immanent, the life of the Spirit is one of diligent work and patient persistence. Many important things do not come easily. We are willing to work hard for the well-being of our families, the sake of our careers, and the secure future of our loved ones. We must be willing to work just as hard for our life with God. It is a question of our very survival with and before him.

Many people who face debilitating diseases have regular and rigorous routines which they must endure just to survive. The procedures or medications may seem time-consuming and painful. Their fruit may not be immediately evident. Yet such measures may be the only thing holding back death.

The same is true of prayer. God tells us we need to do it—so do it we must. Prayer is not a perk, a way of enriching our lives, or a way to make ourselves feel good. It is the way to live faithfully. Only through the disciplines of prayer do we allow God to keep our life focused on his purposes.

But it is always on God's terms. The Tower of Babel reminds us that we cannot reach, control, or manipulate God on our conditions. It is God who reaches out to us. God is inaccessible yet he makes himself accessible to us. Prayer is our response to God's initiative. We do not choose how and where God speaks to us and certainly not what he says.

Our relationship with God is not only about the cozy compatibility of a parent. Our relationship requires disciplines, sometimes even causing pain, the cost of growth. We must be patient before him.

> Our soul waits for the Lord;
> he is our help and shield. (Ps. 33:20)

We want God to be easy and undemanding, but prayer is work. Jesus was often confronted by questions during his ministry, but he seldom answered them directly. This shows that it takes work and patience (and God's Spirit, not simply our abilities or intellect) to gain knowledge of the kingdom of heaven.

We want God to be as simple and accessible as a TV—simply turn it on. Perhaps that is why scandalous televangelists are so successful in their pursuit of wealth: they package a distorted, easy spirituality for TV addicts.

Actually TV—any kind of TV—is a major threat to our spiritual well-being. How much time do we spend before it? And how much time in prayer or worship? Do we pass more time listening to God or watching images that try to sell us cars, cereal, deodorant, or impossibly perfect bodies? Are we more influenced by spirituality or television? Many say they are too busy to pray more, but most are not too busy to watch TV regularly. Are we willing to turn it off for a year, a month, a week, a day, an evening, or even an hour to nourish our lives of prayer, that most vital link between heaven and earth?

The transcendent God in heaven initiates relationship. While inaccessible, he reaches out to us in ways that are often unexpectedly indirect, catching us off guard—a burning bush, a still small voice, a baby in a barn, a convict on a cross.

> O Christ, you are continually worshiped in heaven and on earth, in all times and at all hours; you are patience, compassion and mercy; you love the righteous, you have mercy on sinners, and you call all . . . to salvation, promising them all things to come: receive our prayer, this day . . . and make our life conform to your will; sanctify our souls and our bodies, order our thoughts, and give us victory in all trials and sadness; protect us and bless us, so that we may come to unity of faith and knowledge of your glory, for you live and reign, with the Father and the Holy Spirit, God now and forever.[7]

6

Hallowed Be Thy Name

"Hallowed be your name" (Matthew, Luke: NRSV, NIV, NAB)
"May your name be held holy" (Matthew, Luke: JB)
"Thy name be hallowed" (Matthew, Luke: NEB)

What's in a Name?

The Psalms are full of language about blessing, magnifying, glorifying, praising, and hallowing God's *name*. "O Lord, our Sovereign, how majestic is your *name* in all the earth!" (Ps. 8:1).

At this point in our Lord's Prayer, we are beyond the introduction and salutation. Here we encounter the first petition, the first thing we ask God for—hallowed be your name. This is not something we ask for ourselves. It is a petition we make for and about God. Hallowed be *your* name. May your name be holy.

This petition is directly connected to the next two requests. "Hallowed be your name" equals "your kingdom come" and also equals "your will be done." In fact, as we shall see, the phrase "on earth as it is in heaven" applies to all three of these petitions. Thus we could pray here, "Hallowed be thy name on earth as it is in heaven."

We know, of course, that names are important. One of my wife's co-workers is named "Precious." Can you imagine carrying such a title? Her very name proclaims to the world how important she was to her parents.

Yet we are perhaps casual in naming our children. And we easily and lightly tell each other our names. When people first meet me, they do not know what title to use. In our largely Catholic city of Windsor, some are inclined to call me "Father." And almost no one knows how to pronounce my last name (After all, either "bores" or "boors" might be taken as an insult!).

But my generation is averse to titles, so I often say my name is "just Arthur." No matter how well or poorly people know me, I invite them to call me by my given name. Many people of my generation also choose to be on a first name basis with children. But when I was growing up, I was not permitted such familiarity with adults. They were "Mr.," "Mrs.," or "Miss." I could use first names of special friends of my parents if I preceded their names with *oom* (uncle) or *tante* (aunt).

A friend recently picked up a hitchhiker, a migrant worker from the Caribbean. They had a long drive and a good conversation.

After awhile, the hitchhiker stretched out his hand to my friend and said, "Okay. You're all right. You're a good man. You can know my name. I'm Bob."

In this man's culture, giving one's name suggests a certain intimacy, familiarity, relationship, and trust. In our culture, such feelings might be reserved for intimate pet names or fond nicknames. Often lovers have secret (sometimes silly) names for each other, names no one else knows.

In biblical times, names were even more important than they are today. Names then symbolized the character and essence of a person. Names were never just labels. In such a context, to speak of the name of God is to talk about God's nature, essence, personality, and character. It is an awesome thing to speak of God's name. "God alone has the power to name himself. His name is unpronounceable for human lips."[1]

While humans were once particularly protective of their names, God was and remains even more so. We must never forget that God controls our relationship. He allows some intimacy with him, he grants some access to his name, but it is always on his terms. God encourages our closeness, but this closeness is never at the expense of our reverence and his transcendence.

"And those who know your name put their trust in you," the psalmist says (Ps. 9:10a). This is a different kind of name knowledge than we are accustomed to. Here, knowing God's name indicates a level of relationship that involves trust. "Our pride is in the name of the Lord our God" (Ps. 20:7b). This relationship prevents us from being too friendly, too chummy with God. We may use his name, but only on his terms. God's name is worthy of reverence and hallowing. When Moses asked God for his name, God answered "I am who I am" (Exod. 3:14).

> "This is my name forever,
> and this my title for all generations." (Exod. 3:15b)

In the Old Testament, our Bibles translate as "Lord" the name that the Jews used for God—*YHWH*. The Jews never even said this name, because it was considered too holy. The Jews had a healthy fear, awe, and wonder about God. The people of Israel said to Moses, "You speak to us, and we will listen; but do not let God speak to us, or we will die" (Exod. 20:19b).

Taking God's Name in Vain

Jesus' teaching here is the logical equivalent of one of the Ten Commandments. "You shall not make wrongful use of the name of the Lord your God, for the Lord will not acquit anyone who misuses his name" (Exod. 20:7). Hallowing God's name is the opposite of taking God's name in vain.

I assume most readers resist the vain and casual use of God's name in everyday language. It is hoped that we know better than to use God's name as part of vulgarity, cursing, swearing, or cliché.

Brought up a Calvinist, I was raised with strict warnings against casual phrases such as "Oh, God." Thus as a teenager I was averse to seeing the movie that had that very title. "Oh, my God" and "honest to God" were similarly frowned upon. Even "thank God" was suspect.

In a travel agency, I once overheard a woman boast how well-behaved her kids are. "Thank God," she concluded and then added, "knock on wood." Whom was she thanking, God or wood? An immigrant child, I was told such blasphemies were "Canadian."

Saying "bless you" or "God bless you" when someone sneezes may be questionable. This seems a quaint relic, a practice of a pre-secular age, but it is superstitious. Earlier, people were afraid that sneezing made one vulnerable to demons; this little blessing offered protection.

In George MacDonald's novel, *The Highlander's Last Song*, two young men converse with their mother. The mother asks them to protect someone.

> "In God's name we will!" said Alister.
> "There is no occasion for an oath, Alister!" said his mother.
> "Alister meant it very solemnly," said Ian.
> "Yes, but it was not necessary—least of all to me. The name of our Lord God should lie as a precious jewel in the cabinet of our hearts, to be taken out only at great times and with loving awe."[2]

Our culture could use a healthy dose of Old Testament respect for the name of God.

Familiarity As Vanity

What concerns me more than our society's swearing and vulgarity is the light, trivial, shallow, and cheap ways God's name is used by *believers*. Whenever someone tells me "the Lord did this" or "the Lord told me," my caution lights go on. Some speak of the Lord with reverence and tender respect, but many speak too casually.

We must be careful when we speak of what the Lord did or did not do. We so quickly use God's name to justify ourselves and our deeds. Worse, we exploit God's name to promote narrow ideologies, support sinful lifestyles, or sell products.

One person discusses his disappointment on visiting the 1990 Christian Booksellers Association. He was appalled by Scripture soap, dog sweaters that invited, "Ask my owner about Jesus," and Christian wind socks. He saw bumper stickers and buttons that proclaimed "Beam Me Up, Jesus" or "Born Again in the USA" (the latter using an American flag for background). He even found Bible book playing cards and a Christian workout video. Lamenting such imitation of consumer fads of the world, he suggest a paraphrase of Romans 12:2: "Do not buy any longer the products of this world, but transform them into renewed profits from people of like minds."[3]

God's holy name is trivialized by our casual chatter. Rather than being used to endorse products, God's name is to be guarded and used cautiously. Tatiana Goricheva is a dissident Russian Christian who was exiled in 1980. Arriving in Europe and seeing her first religious broadcast on television, she said,

> I thank God that in Russia we have atheism and no religious education. For the first time I understood how dangerous it is to talk about God. Each word must be a sacrament—filled to the brim with authenticity. Otherwise it is better to keep silent.[4]

God's name is also violated, taken in vain, when used by governments, institutions, or businesses to defend themselves or build themselves up. Thus for example currency that proclaims "In God we trust" is blasphemous.

Late last century, during the Spanish-American War, the United States considered capturing the Philippines and ultimately did so. President McKinley told a group of visiting pastors that he did not want to conquer the Philippines, but God instructed him otherwise.

> I walked the floor of the White House night after night until midnight; and I am not ashamed to tell you, gentlemen, that I went down on my knees and prayed Almighty God for light and guidance more than one night. And one night late it came to me this way . . . that there was nothing left for us to do but to take them all and to educate the Filipinos, and uplift and civilize and Christianize them, and by God's grace do the very best we could by them, as our fellow men for whom Christ also died. And then I went to bed and went to sleep and slept soundly.[5]

McKinley's decision resulted in the slaughter of tens of thousands of Filipinos. Mark Twain ruefully noted, "And so, by these

Providences of God—and the phrase is the government's not mine—we are a World Power."[6]

During the winter of 1991, the world endured the horrific Persian Gulf War. One thing that made this war noteworthy was the fact that the two major personalities of this conflict, George Bush and Saddam Hussein, both claimed to have God on their side. Hussein's claims did not bother me too much as he represents a different faith (although the Muslims I know all tell me that Hussein's faith is only one of political convenience).

But I was dismayed by Bush's claim that he was acting according to Christian faith. I was further appalled by Billy Graham's close association with Bush during this war. (One could not help but remember that Billy Graham seemed to endorse Richard Nixon's conducting of the Vietnamese War as well.)

Driving to church one Sunday, I was shocked to hear that Bush had declared the day a national day of prayer for coalition troops in the Middle East. (He overlooked the fact that Jesus commanded us to love and pray for our enemies.) Who made George Bush a spiritual leader?

Television evangelists saw the war as a fulfillment of biblical prophecy, an instrument that would defeat Islam. Yet so-called Christians had already conducted wars, the Crusades, in the Middle East. Those blasphemous usurpations of God's name still scar the region today.

Some time ago, I met a Canadian missionary who works in a small overseas country ruled by a military dictator. He told me proudly that he is on good terms with the government. In fact, the dictator gave him a huge parcel of land for his ministry. This missionary is regularly invited to preside at and bless government proceedings. There he functions as a chaplain. This left me profoundly uneasy. It seems to me a misuse of blessing.

Eugene L. Davenport reminds us that blessing "is implicitly for the purpose of bringing that person or thing within the scope of God's own holiness, but there are some things that should not be hallowed . . . because they, by nature, oppose the purposes of God."[7] Thus Davenport appropriately condemns the use of God's blessings for beauty pageants, sports events, and most public events.

"God-Language" and Evangelism

Overused God-language is a serious problem in evangelism today. God and Christ have been conscripted to support capitalism, the North American way, Marxism, health food, get-rich-quick schemes, and glamour. These claims discredit the gospel.

People are so overexposed to Christian vocabulary that it all sounds old, very old. John 3:16 has been so often repeated it now sounds as trite as asking, "How are you?" A once-beautiful verse is now empty, void, worn out. Some sports fans wear silly wigs and write John 3:16 on their shirts, hoping to catch the attention of TV cameras. This demeans the gospel, making people tired of Christianity before they have a chance to hear the good news afresh.

The late Walker Percy was sensitive to this. He said that today's Christian writer is

> like a man who . . . after much ordeal and suffering meets an apostle who has the authority to tell him a great piece of news. . . . He . . . runs . . . to tell his countrymen, only to discover that the news has already been broadcast, that this news is in fact the weariest canned spot-announcement on radio-TV, more commonplace than the *Esso* commercial, that in fact he might just as well be shouting *Esso*! *Esso*! for all that anyone pays any attention to him.[8]

By now, God-talk has diverse and distorted meanings, implications, and connotations. Frederick Buechner writes,

> If the language that clothes Christianity is not dead, it is at least, for many, dying; and what is really surprising, I suppose, is that it has lasted as long as it has. . . . There was a time when such words as *faith, sin, redemption,* and *atonement* had great depth of meaning, great reality; but through centuries of handling and mishandling they have tended to become such empty banalities that just the mention of them is apt to turn people's minds off like a switch.[9]

Paul was not disturbed by people wrongly preaching Jesus: "Christ is proclaimed in every way, whether out of false motives or true; and in that I rejoice" (Phil. 1:18). But he wrote in a pre-Christian society. The gospel then was new and stimulating. In our post-Christian context, Christian vocabulary is laden with connotations. Apart from a few immigrants, most North Americans have heard all the gospel clichés many times.

Let us not be so quick to talk about God. Rather than multiplying witnessing opportunities, this only hardens hearts and ears to the good news. We should show the reticence and reverence of the Hebrews who hesitated to say God's name.

Similarly, let us avoid clichés and stop trying to force everything into Four Spiritual Laws. Jesus had no universal formula for salvation. He approached people individually, seldom repeating himself. He only *once* recommended being born again—and that to *one* person. We need to do more than mimic empty God-language.

We need a moratorium on tired and meaningless phrases, such as "accept Jesus as my personal Lord and Savior." Let us instead confess in new and fresh language what Jesus accomplishes. Only as we speak authentically, reporting and proclaiming the marvelous works of God, will we see evangelism break new ground in our society. If our post-Christian context challenges us to let go of cheap clichés, then truly this is an opportunity for God's kingdom.

Named After God

In spite of my aversion to secular abuse of God-language, non-Christians cannot take God's name in vain. Clarence Jordan says one must take on a name before one can take it in vain.

> I can . . . say "Buddha damn" all day long and never take the name of Buddha in vain. I have never taken the name of Buddha. I haven't circulated it around that I am a disciple of Buddha. I cannot take his name in vain. First I have to take it.
>
> Now the words *in vain* mean "empty and meaningless, of no account, of no seriousness." We take it and on we go and it means nothing. We keep sailing under the same old banner, living the same old life, having the same old attitudes, walking in the same old way. The name has meant nothing to us. It doesn't change us. You don't take the name of the Lord in vain with your lips. You take it in vain with your life. It isn't the people outside the church who take God's name in vain. They've never taken it so they can't take it in vain. It's the people on the inside . . . they're the ones

> many times whose lives are totally unchanged by the grace of God. They're the ones who take the name in vain.[10]

Hallowing God's name, then is not only, merely, or even mainly about our words or language or vocabulary. It is primarily about our lives, the way we live. "We reverence God and we hallow God's name, when our life is such that it brings honor to God and attracts others to him."[11] God's name is to be hallowed and glorified in our lives. That is why we are baptized in the *name* of the Father, the Son, and the Holy Spirit.

My son was named after my father. We did not labor over the decision. It is the tradition in my family to name the first son after the husband's father, so we did. But my father's reaction gave me insight into the significance of being named after someone.

My father was preparing to go to the Netherlands around the time Paul was born. He was swamped with work. Yet he managed to fly to Chicago on a Saturday evening, stay overnight, attend church on Sunday morning, and fly home on Sunday afternoon. On Monday, he flew to the Netherlands. Although this made for a hectic schedule, he felt he *had* to see the little person named after him.

God takes just such delight in all Christians named after him. Thus to pray "may your name be held holy" is not just a declaration or affirmation. It states our hope and commitment that God's name be hallowed. Our lives are lived for that purpose. The Westminster Catechism reminds us that our "chief end" is "glorify God and enjoy him forever."

Again there are implications for evangelism here. Nietzche said, "Show me that you are redeemed and then I will believe in your redeemer."[12] The way we live reveals our true beliefs.

I have heard that Karl Rahner said, "The number one cause of atheism is Christians. Those who proclaim God with their mouths and deny him with their lifestyles is what an unbelieving world finds simply unbelievable." Our baptism in God's name calls us to a way of life that permits and allows God to hallow his name through our lives.

7

Thy Kingdom Come

"Thy kingdom come" (Matthew, Luke: RSV, KJV, NEB)
"Your kingdom come" (Matthew, Luke: NRSV, NIV, NAB, JB)

Waiting, Waiting, Always Waiting

Some time ago, I was expecting visitors in my office. I left my door open so they could find me. But that did not help.

I did not notice them as they passed through the hall. They saw me but walked by and explored the rest of the hall. Finally realizing their mistake, they came back. Hesitantly they called through my door, "Boers?"

They were surprised. They did not expect me to be the pastor. "You're so young!" the man exclaimed. (I'm still young enough to be annoyed when people say that I'm so young. I'm always tempted to reply, "I'm older than I look." Soon enough, soon enough, I will want people to tell me I look so young.)

The visiting couple had just arrived as refugees from Vietnam. Thai and Hoa are in their fifties. In their work and involvements at home, they had good experiences with Mennonites and Quakers. They were visiting me because they like Mennonites, even though they themselves are not Christians.

We talked about the troubles in Vietnam. Several of their friends had been arrested or expelled from the country. Believing they too might soon be arrested, Thai and Hoa left. During the war, he was jailed three times and she twice for opposing American-supported dictators. As political prisoners they were never actually charged with anything. He was in jail five years, was an Amnesty International prisoner-of-conscience, and was once released when Senator Edward Kennedy intervened.

We only had a short visit with one another, as we looked for leads for their employment. What sticks with me, though, are their comments about the church in Vietnam. The criticisms these deeply committed people made caught my attention. Thai told me that he is an atheist. His wife, Hoa, is a Buddhist.

The church in Vietnam, they explained, often sided with oppressors. Perhaps 15 percent of the country are Roman Catholics, yet most of the dictators were Catholics who oppressed the Buddhist majority. Thai told of a North American missionary who said, "It is a Christian duty to kill communists."

I liked Thai and Hoa very much. It is little wonder that with their church experiences they are not interested in being Christians. North American missionaries who support dictatorships, persecute people of other faiths, and take it as their duty to kill others deserve blame for that. Such Christians do not know what it means to hallow God's name, to hope for God's kingdom to come, and to work for God's will to be done.

Thus we find ourselves still waiting and longing for God's kingdom to come.

The Centrality of the Kingdom

Again we note that this petition equals the previous and following petitions: "hallowed be thy name" and "thy will be done." Thus we can also render this petition as "thy kingdom come on earth as it is in heaven." The prayer continues to orient us first of all to God's priorities.

This petition was the theme of the first sermon I preached, at age twenty. I perceived then (and still believe now) that the kingdom of God is a central theme of the gospel. I have changed my mind about many things since then, but the centrality of the kingdom of God remains a favorite theme in my life.

The importance of the kingdom is anticipated in the Old Testament. The phrase "kingdom of heaven" or "kingdom of God" is never actually used in the Old Testament, but the idea is found there. Many passages refer to "thy" or "his" (God's) kingdom (Ps. 45:6; 103:19; 145:11-13). The idea of God as king permeates the Old Testament. Thus, for example, we read, "The Lord will reign forever and ever" (Exod. 15:18).

In fact, the Israelites did without a king for a long time because they believed only God, and no human, could be king. After the defeats at the hands of the Assyrians and Babylonians, the Jews hoped for a return to their previous kingdom. Thus the time of Jesus was characterized by hopes for a Messiah who would usher in God's kingdom and vanquish the occupying Romans.

John the Baptist, Jesus, and his disciples all preached, "Repent for the kingdom of heaven has come near" (Matt. 3:2; 4:17; 10:7). Later Philip and Paul preached and testified to the kingdom of God (Acts 8:12; 28:23, 30). Given the centrality of the kingdom to Jesus' preaching and ministry, we can easily conclude that "thy kingdom come" is a petition which informs all the other petitions in the Lord's Prayer.

Kingdom means *reign*. The kingdom of God refers to the reign of God, embracing all that falls under God's rule. God's kingdom has made us into a people (1 Pet. 2:9). Since kingdom often refers to a geographical area, God's *reign, rule* or *kingship* are also good terms to describe what Jesus was talking about.

Here, But Still Coming

The kingdom is a paradoxical reality. In some sense it has already arrived. Jesus said that "in fact, the kingdom of God is among you" (Luke 17:21b). It arrived in truth and power with the life, ministry, death, and resurrection of Jesus Christ. It is among us wherever the will of God is done.

But the kingdom has not *completely* arrived. We pray, "thy kingdom come" because we still wait for it. We still long for God's kingdom to arrive on earth as in heaven. Revelation 11:15

looks forward to the day when angels will proclaim in loud voices, "The kingdom of the world has become the kingdom of our lord and of his Messiah, and he will reign forever and ever."

In significant ways, the kingdom has arrived, is present, is now. It is here, in the midst of us. But in other significant ways the kingdom is future, the kingdom is coming, the kingdom is longed for. How can something be present and future at the same time? How can something be both now and later at the same time? What are we to make of this paradox?

In Chicago, two of our good friends, David and Jill, decided they wanted to buy a house. They started a long and complicated house hunt. We noticed an interesting dynamic. They could not agree on what they were looking for. Were they wanting a *present* house or a *future* house? As they looked at possible properties, the very things that most pleased David most distressed Jill. The things Jill liked were the points that made Dave unhappy.

In our inner city neighborhood, properties could be bought with little money. They were cheap, but they invariably involved a lot of work. Dave, a handy man, enjoyed such a challenge. He likes fixing and rehabbing. So he was attracted to a future house. "Who cares what it looks like now!" He could see, imagine, and envision what the house might someday be. He could at the same time anticipate the joy of getting there.

But Jill would see a house as it was. She knew what it would be like to live in during the in-between time. She knew how long David, the master procrastinator, would take to fix the house. And in the messy meantime, she and the children would cope with the chaos and the incompletion.

Looking at the very same house, they both saw different houses. One saw a present house and the other a future house. Thus a strong negative for one ("This house needs a lot of work," said with resignation) is at the same time a strong positive for the other ("This house needs a lot of work!" said with enthusiastic relish). Perhaps that is a little like the mystery of the kingdom present and the kingdom future.

Our small congregation in Windsor had a similar experience. In 1990, we became the proud owners of an abandoned and decrepit laundromat, ostentatiously named "The Grand Launderette." When we bought the building, we did not just see the building present. Some of us could see the possibility for something new and better—the building future.

When it comes to the future, many of us have a limited imagination, with no idea how to move from a building present to a building future. I remember an early meeting of our congregation's building committee in which we struggled with the tension between the building present and the building future. The technicians among us studied and scrutinized, theorizing and fantasizing with vigorous enthusiasm about the building future.

Meanwhile two women hung back, preoccupied (I suspect) with building present. I asked Linda what she thought of the building, but she avoided a direct answer. "It has potential," she said. At least she was open toward the building future!

The kingdom of God is like that. It is here, it is real, it is solid, it is substantial. But it is not yet complete or fully realized. It is under construction, in process. It still needs some work, vision, grace. It still "has potential."

In the little mountain village of Mombin Crochu, in northeast Haiti, I attended a series of meetings in the local Protestant church building. One part of its wall was open to the outside world, where an unfinished addition lay waiting for needed funds. The building stayed this way for years. That church and its building was (like the kingdom of God itself) real and already contributing to God's purposes, even if not yet completed.

This petition "thy kingdom come" arises from a people who live at the intersection between two kingdoms. "Lord God, thank you that your kingdom arrived among us. But, O Lord, we long for it come fully!" Living in in-between situations is painful and awkward, so we ask for God's alleviation of our discomfort: "thy kingdom come."

The Dominion of God

The kingdom is to be our priority. We are to follow Jesus and live as he directs. "But strive first for the *kingdom* of God and his righteousness, and all these things will be given to you as well" (Matt. 6:33). Since the kingdom is our highest loyalty, we reject the practice of having national flags in our sanctuaries. When I pastored a Methodist church with many Mennonite attenders, one way the Mennonites' convictions were respectfully affirmed was by removing the national flag from the sanctuary.

While we may be comfortable with the rejection of worldly patriotism, obedience and submission is not a popular notion now. For example, as a child I often heard the word *dominion*. Our nation was called the *Dominion* of Canada. On July 1, we celebrated Dominion Day.

But the term has fallen into disfavor and disuse.[1] In 1982, our patriotic celebration became Canada Day rather than *Dominion* Day. Our nation is now commonly referred to as just plain Canada. Thus, for example, the Dominion Bureau of Statistics is now called Statistics Canada.

I am not too concerned about this change of vocabulary regarding my own country. But I suspect it reflects a spirit of individualism. We resist the idea of an explicit dominion requiring our obedience and submission. Gordon MacDonald notes that the United States has a bias against anything royal. He thinks this contributes to an American inability to exercise due reverence for God.[2]

Despite our biases against monarchs and tyrants (usually appropriate!), despite the unpopularity of such notions as *dominion*, this petition specifically calls us to obey God. "Therefore, since we are receiving a kingdom that cannot be shaken, let us give thanks, by which we offer to God an acceptable worship with reverence and awe" (Heb. 12:28-29).

In praying this petition, we hear the call to faithful obedience, which means already living the future kingdom now. We are called to live differently than the world, even as we live in the world. Thus our way of life, our priorities, and our values are different than the world's. We are never completely at home here.

To pray this petition sincerely means that our goals become geared according to God's goals. We do not seek success, wealth, prestige, or fame. Rather, we seek first his kingdom and his righteousness. A friend, Paul Uptigrove, once pointed out that to pray for God's kingdom is to become subversives (perhaps even revolutionaries). Like other committed revolutionaries, we deny ourselves for the cause of the kingdom, we love the kingdom more than anything else, and we are prepared to give up everything for the sake of the kingdom.

We are like a tired traveler I once read about. At the time of the article, he had already lived for two years with only his weekend bag in Paris' Charles DeGaulle airport.[3] Alfred Merhan, forty-five years old, lost his Iranian citizenship in the 1970s when he participated in London protests against the late Shah of Iran. He eventually received stateless status from Belgium.

During a two-day trip to Paris, he was robbed of his documents. Since then, he has been unable to persuade any government to give him official status. He has a plane ticket to London, but because of his uncertain status he may not fly. He is stuck in the departure zone. (One might consider this a plot for the "Twilight Zone!") As Christians, we are in a similarly ambivalent relationship with the world: we are *in* but do not *belong* to it.

To pray about God's kingdom is to pray about today and now, because indeed the kingdom has come. But it is also to pray about the future, for the kingdom is yet to come. To pray "thy kingdom come" is to hope for God's kingdom, to long for it. In some senses, it is to long for the end of the world. But when we long for the end of the world, we really mean (in the words of an old cliché) "the end of civilization as we know it." We mean the end of our world's values and the success of the kingdom's values. We long for the time when Jesus Christ, King of kings and Lord of the universe, is completely obeyed.

We often get mixed up in such longings. Sometimes when the world looks bad, we wish God would come and demolish it: "I wish the Lord would return." I am embarrassed to admit that during high school, when particularly worried about exams, I used to hope that the world would end before I had to write my exams! Some people respond to any stress, problems, or crises by sighing, "I wish the Lord would hurry up and return."

Once I attended a forum on the Christian response to nuclear weapons. I was shocked when a Mennonite preacher said that to pray, "thy kingdom come," is to pray for nuclear war. This, he said, is because nuclear war would end the world and usher in God's kingdom. I disagree.

No, to pray "thy kingdom come" is to long for the coming of God's kingdom. It is the equivalent of the martyrs' prayer: "Sovereign Lord, holy and true, *how long* will it be . . . " (Rev. 6:10a). It echoes John: "Amen. Come, Lord Jesus!" (Rev. 22:20b) and Paul's exclamation: "Our Lord, come!" (1 Cor. 16:22).

When I first approached this text, I intended to write only about how this prayer is a call to be loyal and true to God's kingdom. I wanted to write mostly about the need for our obedience to do God's work. That is all true, but I now also see that this prayer is a cry of hope and yearning, a sigh of longing, even a despairing plea . . . all rooted in God's hope.

To be in-between is painful. Like the departure zone hostage, we get tired, frustrated, discouraged. We want to have arrived. We want to see the building complete and whole. We want God's kingdom fully among us. Instead we live the reality that while the kingdom has indeed arrived, it is not yet complete. In this in-between reality we pray, "thy kingdom come."

Some years ago, I received a mysteriously cryptic telephone call. Sadly, I got confused about being between two kingdoms.

"I wonder if you can help me?" asked a woman who did not identify herself. "Do you have a banquet room?"

"We don't even have a church building yet," I responded.

"Oh, thank-you." She hung up and the line went dead.

But I still wonder whether I handled the call wrongly. She wanted a banquet room. The Bible often describes God's kingdom as a feast, a banquet. At the time, our church did not even have a building, let alone a banquet room. But every time we gather, we have a banquet. When we share refreshments, we anticipate God's banquet. Each fellowship meal and every communion is an anticipation of the kingdom to come.

Maybe I should have told her: "We have no building, not yet. But God's coming kingdom has already arrived!"

I can only echo Bonhoeffer's prayer. "God grant that the kingdom of Jesus Christ may grow in his Church on earth, God hasten the end of the kingdoms of this world, and establish his own kingdom in power and glory!"[4]

8

Thy Will Be Done

"Thy will be done" (Matthew: RSV, KJV, NEB)
"Your will be done" (Matthew: NRSV, NIV, NAB, JB)

The Poetry of Parallels

"I delight to do your will, O my God;
your law is within my heart." (Ps. 40:8)

The Psalms seem like poetry to us, even though they have been translated into English—and do not rhyme in either language. In fact, Hebrew poetry is not based on rhyming but on parallels. In this kind of poetry, statements are made and then restated in a way that broadens understanding.

The Hebrew poet says something and then repeats it in slightly different words. For example,

He who sits in the heavens laughs;
the Lord has them in derision. (Ps. 2:4)

Or,

He will make your vindication shine like the light,
and the justice of your cause like the noonday. (Ps. 37:6)

Jesus, in the tradition of Hebraic poetry, also used such repetition.

> Ask, and it will be given you;
> search, and you will find;
> knock, and the door will be opened for you. (Matt. 7:7)

And he specifically used triplicate parallelism in our Lord's Prayer.

> Hallowed be your name.
> Your kingdom come.
> Your will be done. (Matt. 6:9-10)

Each phrase parallels the other. They relate to the will of God, the petition we are presently looking at. When God's will is done, the kingdom comes. Note that this petition, "thy will be done" is only found in Matthew's version of this prayer. (The King James Version does include it in Luke too.)

The Will of God in Life's Difficult Circumstances

When I hear the petition "thy will be done," I see in my memory's eye a funeral card. It was given to mourners at one of the most tragic funerals I ever attended. A young friend died of AIDS, leaving behind a widow and a little child who were both HIV positive. The phrase struck me then and I wondered, was that God's will?

This petition is often linked with a cliché that we insert into our prayers: "not our will, but thy will be done." Partly, we echo Jesus' desperate prayer in the garden—"not my will but yours be done" (Luke 22:42). At such times we are also mindful of John's advice: "And this is the boldness we have in him, that if we ask anything according to his will, he hears us" (1 John 5:14). Yet these are hard words to utter, possibly, "the most difficult line in the entire prayer to pray."[1]

It is impossible to read the Bible and be totally objective. Whatever is going on in our own lives will inevitably influence *what* we choose to read or *how* we read whatever we happen to be reading. Thus the events of my life always affect my reading of a biblical text. Experience always impacts our perspective.

The first time that I wrestled deeply with this text and tried to study it, my father was diagnosed as having lung cancer. At the time we had no idea of the cancer's seriousness and had to await his surgery to know what would happen.

What does it mean to pray "thy will be done" now? I wondered. What does this mean as I worry about my own father? What does it mean, when I know that my parents aren't sleeping well because they do not know what the future holds? What does it mean to pray, hope, and long for my father's health and at the same time pray "thy will be done"?

The faith I grew up with espoused a fatalistic idea of predestination. God predestined everything, therefore what will happen will happen. As that great "theologian" Doris Day used to sing, "*Que sera, sera*" (Whatever will be, will be). "You never go before your time." For some, there is comfort in such beliefs. "Thy will be done" is then about fate. For me this is inadequate.

The will of God is a phrase we casually toss about. But do we really know what it means? In high school, I worried about God's will for my life. What kind of work should I pursue? Would I marry? How, where, and when might I find my spouse?

A saintly man once preached to some of us youth. Reflecting on Abraham's story, he insisted God had a plan for our lives. If we paid attention to God, we would learn the three important "p's": profession, place, and person (spouse). I was comforted by his words then, although I no longer agree with him.

"God loves you and has a wonderful plan for your life," we used to say confidently. But it is often hard to see that plan or the plan does not always look too wonderful. Even so, I still treasure the preacher's words for giving me one true assurance: God loves us in the particular details and circumstances of our lives.

"Thy will be done" is not a prayer of resignation or a passive acceptance of fate. It really means something far different. At the tragic funeral, I could not say that that untimely death was God's will. It was not God's will that my friend die of AIDS, nor was it God's will that his innocent wife and child be infected with the likely possibility of AIDS. God is not like that.

Once I was called in on an emergency. A woman was worried about her brother, who had a long history of serious problems. He was not answering the phone. When we went to his apartment, he did not answer the door. Although it was locked, we managed to get in. We found him in bed. His eyes were open, but he was unresponsive. He had not washed, shaved, or groomed for days. Overdosed on after shave lotion and aspirin, he was unable to take care of himself. We called an ambulance.

As I sat by his bed, trying to speak with him and waiting for the ambulance, I did not pray, "Thy will be done." I certainly did not think, *Thy will is being done now*. I do not believe it was God's will for that fellow to hurt himself. Nor was it God's will that his family suffer so on his behalf.

To understand this petition, we must look elsewhere.

I Did It God's Way

God wills that we lead a life befitting the kingdom of God, a life in obedience to God. The will of God (as we pray for it here in our Lord's Prayer) refers to the purposes of God. He intends that today, here and now, we live in the promise of heaven. He intends that we follow him.

Thus God's will for my dead friend would have been for him to have lived in service to God, not service to himself. I remember visiting him once, long before I knew of his disease. He said he wanted to be a lawyer so he could make lots of money. I asked why he wanted to make lots of money.

He grinned in embarrassment, "I knew you'd ask that."

But he did not answer my question. Only two and a half years later, he died and never attained the goal of making lots of money. That memory makes his death even more tragic.

God's will for my overdosed acquaintance was that he learn to love himself, his neighbor, and God. God's will for my father is that he walk faithfully with God, on both sides of the grave. God's will, his purpose for us, is that we live in obedience to him.

" 'Your will be done' is not an assertion that everything which happens is God's will. It is, in fact, a plea that recognizes God's will is not done on earth."[2] To pray "thy will be done" is to long for things to change. It is to hope that no one else will suffer or die from AIDS. It is to yearn for self-abusing people to be freed from the bondage of addictions and self-destruction. To pray "thy will be done" is to long for the day when God dwells with us, the day when

> he will wipe every tear from their eyes.
> Death will be no more;
> mourning and crying and pain will be no more,
> for the first things have passed away. (Rev. 21:4)

Thy will be done on earth as in heaven is a prayer that does not merely resign itself to suffering. It is not God's will that people suffer. God's will is that heaven's joy, comfort, and consolation might be fully known on earth.

In the meantime, in this between time, we live at the intersection between the kingdom present and the kingdom to come (as we saw in our last chapter). Thus we are here and now faced with how we will respond to God and his will. Will we follow and obey him? Or will we lead our lives as if God and his purposes and his intentions are not important?

I am told that C. S. Lewis said there are only two kinds of people in the world—those who say to God "thy will be done," and those whom God says "thy will be done." Which do we choose? Do we do things our way, as that other great "theologian" Frank Sinatra likes to sing? Or are we willing to let God have his way?

"Thy will be done" is a phrase central to all of Jesus' life.

> My food is to do the *will* of him who sent me and to complete *his work*. (John 4:34)
> I can do nothing on my own. As I hear, I judge; and my judgment is just, because I seek to do not my own will but the *will* of him who sent me. (John 5:30)
> For I have come down from heaven, not to do my own will, but the *will* of him who sent me. (John 6:38)

As we have already noted, during the greatest crisis of his life, Jesus also prayed about God's will: "My Father, if this cannot pass unless I drink it, *your will be done*" (Matt. 26:42).

Some Christians are content to talk about their faith. But belief and faith cannot be separated from faithful obedience. Our beliefs bear fruit in deeds and actions. We often hear the term *born again* from various translations of John 3:3. The Greek word (*anōthn*) literally means "born from above." It means obeying the will of our heavenly God here on earth. We "were born, not of blood or of the will of the flesh or of the will of man, but of God" (John 1:13). Such obedience qualifies us to be part of Jesus' family.

> While he was still speaking to the crowds, his mother and his brothers were standing outside, wanting to speak to him. Someone told him, "Look, your mother and your brothers are standing outside, wanting to speak to you." But to the one who had told him this, Jesus replied, "Who is my mother, and who are my brothers?" And pointing to his disciples, he said, "Here are my mother and my brothers! For whoever does the will of my Father in heaven is my brother and sister and mother." (Matt. 12:46-50)

Praying the Lord's Prayer to "our Father in heaven" entails an obedience to do God's will. We do not just pray that God will do his will; we commit ourselves to that will. And that commitment enables us to call God our "Father" and Jesus our "brother."

The Difficulty of Obeying God

Yet obedience is not easy and we cannot do it on our own. We may choose to be faithful, to follow Jesus. But then we still find ourselves sinning and unable to live up to God's standards. I have long thought that if we truly believed in God and believed that Jesus is the ultimate reality, he would determine all our priorities. Then we would easily orient all our lives to God's priorities. Thus as a pastor I am frustrated when I think that God has a low priority in people's lives. And I think, "If they really and truly believed, they would live differently."

As a parent, I see that it is hard for us to believe and obey. In watching my children, I better understand my own relationship with God. I am a prevailing reality in their lives and they are constantly aware of me. Yet time and again, they do not listen to me. They disobey and break rules. Often and usually they foolishly do this in my presence. Sometimes after being reprimanded for something, they immediately go and repeat the very same offense! The urge to disobey is deep within us.

As a child, my father often got into trouble. When he remembered his disobedient adventures, he included this refrain: "I knew it was wrong. I knew it would get me into trouble. I knew my parents would find out. I knew they would be angry. I knew they would punish me and possibly punish me severely. But I couldn't help myself. I had to do it."

Just so, even if we really do believe in God, we often feel we cannot help ourselves. Like disobedient children, we still sin and still find it difficult to obey God. That is why we also need a petition which comes later in this prayer, the petition of forgiveness. When we pray "thy will be done," we also beg and plead with God to help us be obedient.

Like stubborn children, we do not necessarily want to know the will of our Father. Thus this prayer is difficult. This is not how we really want our life to be. We do not want God to be the boss. *We* want to be the boss. If God does not obey us, look out!

Two days a week, I am home alone working upstairs in my study. I am there when my daughter Erin returns from school. I hear her come through the front door and I call down, "Hi, Erin. How are you? How was school?" Then I say either "I'm up here and will be right down" or "Come on up." Often, she does not bother to say anything or to respond to me.

One day I said nothing when she arrived at home. I may have been too immersed in my work or perhaps I was tired of calling down when she said nothing. Within seconds, she burst into my room, peeved that I had said nothing. She could regularly ignore me, but I had better not ignore her! Sometimes we treat God the same way. We feel free to ignore him but get angry with him the first time he does not meet our expectations.

Obedience to God's will is central to prayer. As I argued in a previous book, *On Earth As in Heaven*, prayer means approaching God on God's terms, not ours. Otherwise prayer is merely magical, misleading us into thinking that we can manipulate God. But that makes God subservient to our prayers. True prayer is summed up in today's petition—"thy will be done."

Dom Hélder Câmara says, "You know the prayer I love to say?

'Lord, may your grace help me to want what you want, to prefer what you prefer.' "[3] The Jewish scholar Gamaliel used to teach, "Do his will as thy will, that he may do thy will as his will."

How serious are we when we pray "thy will be done"? Do we really want this? Are we able to sing *with integrity* the lyrics of this old hymn?

> Have thine own way, Lord
> Have thine own way.
> Thou art the potter,
> I am the clay.

What are we willing to do for God's will? To commit our lives wholly to God's purposes? To be disciplined for him? To live and share the good news? To spread the kingdom of God? To participate wholeheartedly in a local congregation? To support other believers and commit our resources of time and money to God's kingdom, God's will?

Some time ago, I attended an amazing exhibition of akaido, a martial art. It was foreign to me. I was impressed by a little seventy-five year old Japanese man adept at resisting and repelling attackers. He managed to pin four healthy and vital young men without doing them any physical harm or damage.

What impressed me most about the exhibition was the tremendous discipline of the dozens upon dozens of Windsorites there. They were willing to do hard training for several hours a week. They paid much money for lessons, equipment, and uniforms. They submitted to the discipline of their martial art.

I was running low on energy that day, somewhat discouraged about the slow results of pastoring. Were there, I wondered, in all Windsor, as many Christians who would commit themselves like that to the work and discipline of God's kingdom?

The Peril of Self-Righteousness

Sometimes we so emphasize obedience and faithfulness that we become judgmental. Mennonites stress obedience and are thus particularly prone to temptations of self-righteousness.

A friend, Larry Willms, has spent much time in Central America. He was in Nicaragua during the controversial 1990 elections when the Sandinista government was defeated. In a personal newsletter, he wrote of the sixty-year-old Nicaraguan woman, Sophia, who shared her house with international volunteers.

An American woman, Sally, also lived with Sophia around this time. She was militantly pro-Sandinista and would only live with Sophia if Sophia professed to be pro-Sandinista as well.

On the night of the elections, Sally stayed out all night. Sophia, a loving and caring woman, fretted about Sally. At four a.m., she went out to search for Sally. She found Sally with another group of international volunteers. Sally was in despair because of the elections and was weeping uncontrollably. Sophia on the other hand was delighted to find Sally safe. But Sally concluded that Sophia was not really distressed by the election and therefore was not a true pro-Sandinista.

In a huff, Sally moved out of Sophia's home. She could not bear to live with someone who was not pro-Sandinista. Larry wrote, "Sophia was crushed by this, and felt that [Sally] never understood how much she cared about her. On many occasions Sophia would cry, as she and I were eating supper, about how hurt she felt that Sally had left her."

Sally self-righteously felt her politics were correct. (In theological terms, she knew the will of God.) Sally could not abide the presence of someone who perhaps disagreed with her, not even someone who loved and needed her. This in spite of the fact that Sophia is the Nicaraguan and has far more at stake in Nicaraguan politics than Sally, the American. Unfortunately, we Christians are often just as prone to write off those who do not match our expectations.

The will of God is that we be obedient. But we are not to exclude and write off other people. The will of God is that all should find their way with God. Jesus said,

> What do you think? If a shepherd has a hundred sheep, and one of them has gone astray, does he not leave the ninety-nine on the mountains and go in search of the one that went astray? And if he finds it, truly I tell you, he rejoices over it more than over the ninety-nine that never went astray. So it is not the will of your Father in heaven that one of these little ones should be lost. (Matt. 18:12-14)

God's will is that none should be lost. "And this is the will of him who sent me, that I should lose nothing of all that he has given me, but raise it up on the last day" (John 6:39). God loves us precisely as the Good Shepherd of Jesus' parable.

To love those who go astray, who are not obedient and not committed, is to bear a cross. Thus to pray "thy will be done" is about suffering. But it is not just about any *suffering;* it is not about calamity or disease or addiction. It is not about my friend dying of AIDS, or my acquaintance suffering from self-abuse, or my father having cancer. To pray this prayer is not about *fate,* not about *que sera sera.*

The suffering connected to the will of God is the suffering of the cross, the suffering of obedience. That is why Jesus referred to this prayer before his crucifixion (Matt. 26:42; Luke 22:42). Thus the Bible teaches, "For it is better to suffer for doing good, if suffering should be God's will, than to suffer for doing evil" (1 Pet. 3:17).

The early Anabaptists had an important word, *gelassenheit.* It means being yielded and surrendered to God's will. It includes the possibility that one will have to suffer for God's purposes.

Gelassenheit means "thy will be done." It means to make God's will our priority, our most important goal. Hans Denck asserted, "There is no other way to blessedness than to lose one's self will."[4] He also said, "If man shall become one with God, he has to suffer what God intends to work in him."[5] Likewise, Michael Sattler wrote from his prison cell, "In this peril I completely *surrendered* myself unto the will of the Lord, and . . . prepared myself even for death for His testimony."[6]

Similarly, Hans van Overdam wrote from prison in 1550,

> We would rather through the grace of God suffer our temporal bodies to be burned, drowned, racked, or tortured, as it may seem good to you, or be scourged, banished, or driven away, or robbed of our goods, than to show any obedience contrary to the word of God, and we will be patient therein.[7]

These brave and daring sentiments were deeply rooted in the biblical witness: "And the world and its desire are passing away, but those who do *the will of God* live forever" (1 John 2:17).

9

On Earth As in Heaven

"On earth as it is in heaven" (Matthew: NRSV, RSV, NIV, NAB)
"On earth as in heaven" (Matthew: NEB, JB)

The Axis of the Lord's Prayer

Bear with me as I rephrase the Lord's Prayer.

> Our Father who art in heaven,
> Hallowed be thy name, on earth as in heaven.
> Thy kingdom come, on earth as in heaven.
> Thy will be done, on earth as in heaven.
> Give us this day our daily bread, on earth as in heaven.
> And forgive us our debts in heaven,
> as we also have forgiven our debtors on earth.
> And lead us not into temptation on earth,
> but deliver us from evil, on earth as in heaven.
> For thine is the kingdom, the power, and the glory,
> forever and ever. Amen!

You may be surprised to see an entire chapter on a little phrase found only in Matthew, "on earth as in heaven." Perhaps you assumed it was already covered in previous chapters.

But this small phrase strikes me as ever more significant. It is a chorus and refrain that is at the very heart of our Lord's Prayer and indeed of the gospel as a whole. "On earth as in heaven" is the axis around which the whole prayer revolves.

In this phrase, we turn from a heavenward gaze (hallowed be thy name, thy kingdom come) to an earthward gaze. Having addressed God in his glory and majesty, we now turn to specific earthly concerns. We on earth pray for daily bread, forgiveness, deliverance, and protection from evil.

It is as if we say, "If God's name were hallowed, if God's kingdom came, if God's will were done, *then* we on earth would all receive our daily bread, our debts would be forgiven, we would resist temptation, we would be saved from evil." The petitions that follow this phrase show what happens when God's will is done *on earth* as in heaven.

As I researched the Lord's Prayer, most resources had little to say about this phrase. But it reframes the whole prayer. It links two sets of concerns that many often separate. It connects spiritual concerns about God with earthly realities.

Heaven and Earth

We distinguish between heaven and earth, but in God's purposes they are intrinsically related. They are both mentioned in the Bible's first verse: "In the beginning . . . God created the heavens and the earth" (Gen. 1:1). God then turned responsibility for creation over to humanity. The earth was intended as our domain, just as God has his own domain.

> The heavens are Lord's heavens,
> but the earth he has given to human beings. (Ps. 115:16)

In the Bible, "heaven and earth" refers to the whole universe. God is "Lord of heaven and earth." (Matt. 11:25)

> But in comparison with earth, heaven is nearer to the Creator; . . . heaven is God's throne (Matt. 5:34f.) and the earth is his footstool. So the earth is subordinate to heaven. . . . Both are equally parts of the [universe], because both have been created by the one God and are therefore subject to him, but also . . . both are transitory; for "heaven and earth will pass away." (Matt. 5:18; 24:35)[1]

Heaven is the place where God's will is completely obeyed. "Earth is the place where the will of God is still opposed, where God exercises his historical magnanimity and patience."[2] On earth we endure brokenness, sin, and failure. But God has designs on earth: he intends for it to reflect heaven. "May the kingdom that is already victorious in heaven be also established on earth!"[3]

Heaven and earth are separate. We humans cannot move freely between heaven and earth. Only God and his angels can do that. The best we can do is create lives of obedience on earth, lives that point toward the reality of heaven, lives rewarded with the gift of heaven.

Heavenly Aspirations

> Once in heaven, we cannot come back to earth. In the parable of the rich man and Lazarus (Luke 16:19-31), Lazarus goes to heaven but cannot minister to the rich man nor can he return to earth to warn others. This phrase "on earth as in heaven" shows "that heaven and earth are still separate, or at least different . . . and so it asks for this difference to be abolished at the end of time."[4]

We who live on this side of the grave know little about heaven. We know only what God has told us. What the Bible says about heaven can be summarized in a few pages. Heaven is far beyond our imagination, far beyond our grasp, far beyond our vocabulary. Even if we knew of the glories of heaven, words could not convey them.

Heaven is important. But the attention we pay to heaven is often misfocused. I hear, particularly among certain evangelists, a great *anxiety* about whether we will *get* to heaven. Many evangelism methods frighten people into choosing heaven. Such concerns seem understandable, but I do not find justification for them in the Bible.

Growing up in the church of my childhood, people worried about whether they were going to heaven. No one knew for sure. (Mixing in more evangelical circles later in life, I heard people speak calmly about the "assurance of salvation.") As a child, no one I knew felt calm about the prospects of heaven. Yet I do not find this anxiety in the New Testament. Issues that bother us today did not trouble the first believers.

While the Christians I know now are more prone to speak about the "assurance of salvation," I often hear them worry about whether or not certain late relatives went to heaven or hell. The New Testament was written for a first generation of Christians. Presumably many of those believers had relatives who did not profess Christ. Yet the New Testament never addresses such anxiety about heaven. Admittedly, it is risky arguing from silence. But that omission is interesting given our struggles and concerns.

Heaven should not cause such anxiety among us, either. We need to trust that whatever God chooses to do, we will ultimately understand his righteous compassion.

A Paradoxical Passport to Heaven

Paul was so free of worry about going to heaven that he could say in Romans 9:3, "For I could wish that I myself were accursed and cut off from Christ for the sake of my own people, my kindred according to the flesh." Paul was willing to be damned that others might be saved.

Paul's attitude is precisely what Jesus commends. "For those who want to save their life will lose it and those who lose their life for my sake, and for the sake of the gospel, will save it" (Mark 8:35). In the parable of the sheep and the goats (Matt. 25), those who think they deserve heaven are condemned. Those who do not worry about heaven and are anonymously and unconsciously obedient are the ones saved!

There are strangely paradoxical dynamics here.

> You do not love God so that, tit for tat, he will then save you. To love God is to be saved. . . .
>
> You do not love God and live for him so you will go to Heaven. Whichever side of the grave you happen to be talking about, to love God and live for him *is* Heaven.[5]

Much of our preoccupation with heaven is selfish. Persuading people to convert just to avoid hell appeals only to narrow and alas, sinful interests. Søren Kierkegaard wrote, "The man who only wills the Good out of fear of punishment does not will one thing. He is double-minded."[6]

Do we advocate being nice to parents just to inherit something from them? Do I commend my parents to others because they might leave me a legacy? Of course not. Why then do we "sell" being obedient to God to inherit eternal life?

Paradoxically, the passport to heaven includes not even aiming or trying for heaven! We get to heaven by not obsessively aiming at heaven. Ironically, it is when we trust God and cease worrying about consequences that we experience his greatest blessings.

This is reminiscent of the training people take to see during the night. The problem is that the center of the eye is blind in the dark. Thus looking directly at the sound of something during the night will not necessarily show you anything. So one must look to *either side* of the sound—*then* one can see! We only catch a glimpse of heaven if we do not look at it directly.

A friend of mine recently graduated from teacher's college. In a declining economy, she arranged numerous job interviews. She went to her first interview confident she would *not* be offered a job. But she felt it would be a good experience and exercise, a dry run for future interviews. Because she knew the interview was not serious, she was relaxed and unworried. She did not even dress for the interview. She was not trying to get this job. Of course she was offered it. She was so surprised she did not even know how to respond!

Jesus warns that those who are sure of their salvation are in fact condemned. And those who are unsure of salvation are often saved. We cannot make neat and precise formulas about who gets into heaven. Nor should we expend too much energy on such endeavors. As the old cliché goes, "Some people are so heavenly minded, that they do no earthly good."

Heaven's Designs on Earth

In Haiti, Christians complained to me of missionaries who "preached resignation and promised that someday we will have a nice palace." Heaven does not give everyone hope. In Wendell Berry's novel, *A Place on Earth*, a pastor tries to comfort a grieving family with the promise of heaven. But he fails. The father rebukes him, "I can only be comforted by the hope of earth."[7]

Jesus does not want us to focus on heaven, although heaven is important. Nor does he want us only to focus on earth, although earth is important too. He inextricably links and connects the priorities we would separate. The mystery and paradox of the Lord's Prayer is this. It urges us first to focus heavenward, on the things that are God's (his holy name, his kingdom, his will) so we will be passionate about things of this earth.

Focusing on God's concerns and priorities, we naturally embrace the needs of *earth*. As we pray for the hallowing of God's name, the coming of God's kingdom, the doing of God's will, we will also be involved with the distribution of daily bread, forgiveness of sins, deliverance from evil on *earth*. Even then our gaze returns to heaven, to God's kingdom, power, and glory.

Contemporary anxiety about heaven is not biblical. The Lord's Prayer addresses our most important and most basic needs. Nowhere does it say, "Let me get to heaven." But it does ask God's help for living on earth, because temporal life *on earth* has eternal implications. I agree with John Stoner when he asserts that

> the goal of life is not basically to get to heaven; it is to walk with God. Our vocation is to walk with God in caring for his good creation. The direction of God's saving work has always been toward this earth.[8]

We cannot bring ourselves closer to heaven. We can only faithfully obey the God who will bring us closer to heaven so heaven radiates from us. It is not God's intention that heaven and earth remain eternally separate. Thus God speaks from heaven to us on earth. Thus our earthly prayers are heard in heaven. Thus Jesus came from heaven to live on earth. There are many connections between heaven and earth.

More than that, God has designs on earth. He wants to conquer the earth and reclaim it for his purposes. Heaven intends to invade and convert the earth. Heaven is coming down. Heaven is trying to get in here (and will ultimately succeed). But earthly attempts to get to heaven (the Tower of Babel) always fail.

God did not put us on earth for a while to test us and see whether or not we rate heaven. God put us here to enjoy him and his creation and to do his work. He put Christians on earth as a colony or a subversive fifth column of his kingdom. Earth is not just a way station. God intends to take over the earth, and we are representatives in that task.

Heaven is the place where God's intentions are perfectly fulfilled, where his name is hallowed, his kingdom comes, his will is done. God has those perfect intentions for earth as well. We live on the earth as citizens of heaven, trying to implement the priorities of heaven, awaiting the day of heaven's arrival.

> Then I saw a new heaven and a new earth; for the first heaven and the first earth had passed away, and the sea was no more. And I saw the holy city, the new Jerusalem, coming down out of heaven from God, prepared as a bride adorned for her husband. (Rev. 21:1-2)

A City Called Heaven

To live this prayer is to be surrounded by echoes of those old gospel songs which called us to begin living now in the city called heaven.

I recently read about a famous British mountain climber, Mo Anthoine, whom some regard as Britain's greatest climber. He has climbed in Britain, the Alps, Alaska, the Andes, and the Himalayas. But contrary to what many might think, he is not concerned about reaching mountain peaks.

> I don't think getting to the top is all that important. You can always have another go. The things you remember after a trip are not standing on the summit but what went on while you were on route. The nicest feeling is to know that you're relying on someone else and he is relying absolutely on you.[9]

Anthoine's expedition philosophy says that "a trip with great blokes wholly outranks getting to the top."[10]

Let us enjoy our trip with great blokes. Let God worry about getting us to heaven. That's God's job. Let us rather enjoy what

God puts before us now, for this time being. Then we can invite others to that trip as well, to be people of the way, people on the way. Our journey is itself important.

From time to time, we on earth catch glimpses of heaven out of the corners of our eyes. It may be a rousing time of worship, an intimate moment of fellowship, a friend who hears and helps us in times of need, a beautiful scene from God's creation. These glimpses and previews of heaven are meant to be savored.

John describes the new reality of the time when God dwells fully among us—every tear wiped away, death is no more, mourning, crying, and pain does not exist (Rev. 21:4). In the parable of the rich man and Lazarus, poor Lazarus gets to rest in the bosom of Abraham. This is an astonishing image of comfort, reassurance, and intimacy. Once alone, once cold, once hungry. But in heaven he knows complete intimacy, acceptance, warmth, and satisfaction.

Field of Dreams is a beautiful film (even if it is about baseball!). One character regrets a broken relationship with his father. Their alienation is symbolized by something that happened when the son was a teen. He refused to play catch with his dad. A cool teenager, he rejected his father. But his father died before they could make up. Then in a heaven set in an Iowa baseball field, father and son are brought back together and given another chance. Reunited, they play catch together.

That is a fantasy, but it seems profound to me. For heaven is the place where all brokenness will be mended, where we can be reconciled, where all sin is forgiven, where healing happens. And to pray "on earth as in heaven" is to say that we already work for God's reconciliation here on earth. And someday, someday, we will be able to sing with the angels.

> Holy, holy, holy is the Lord of hosts;
> the whole earth is full of his glory. (Isa. 6:3)

10

Our Daily Bread

"Give us this day our daily bread" (Matthew: RSV, NRSV, KJV)
"Give us today our daily bread" (Matthew: NIV, NEB, NAB, JB)
"Give us each day our daily bread" (Luke: RSV, NRSV, NIV, NEB, NAB, JB)
"Give us day by day our daily bread" (Luke: KJV)

Lifestyles of the Rich and Foolish

A nurse who used to work with my wife won a $25,000 lottery. While people congratulated her, she complained, "The IRS takes too much in taxes. If I won a million dollars, *then* I'd be happy."

Some time ago, Lorna and I attended an affluent wedding reception on the other side of the border. The event cost tens of thousands of dollars. We dined in a fancy building overlooking Lake St. Clair. One fellow there, a little younger than I, told me about his thirty-six foot yacht, complete with tower (I don't know what a tower is) but still in need of air conditioning.

This same man also told me of how he once traveled by jet from Detroit to the Bahamas for a one-day junket. He could not go to the beach as it was raining that day. "So I just gambled all day. That was all right!" he said. Another person at the wedding told me of making one-day junkets to Atlantic City, flying there from Detroit for a day's worth of gambling.

I was confused by these men. I could not believe or understand their extravagantly selfish waste of money. Lorna tells me they expected me to be impressed. I wasn't.

I know a man who has a fleet of half a dozen exotic cars. Three of the cars are worth more than $200,000. He likes to complain about the high cost of insurance. I'm sorry to know the details of his spending.

The people I have described here are exceptional. They have too much money. They give little thought to the inequity of their lifestyle. I am almost sorry to have met these people.

Why?

I don't want to be judgmental. Jesus loved and mingled with rich people. He even loved the rich young ruler who turned down Jesus (Matt. 19:21). The Bible often condemns wealth, often warns the wealthy, and even calls some wealthy people foolish. But I am in no position to judge. I am tempted to feel self-righteous and to pontificate about obscenely filthy riches. But I pray that God will not let me succumb to such judgmentalism.

Why then am I sad to know such people? Not (I hope) because I am jealous. Who needs such wealth? If I wanted to be wealthy, I would pursue a different vocation. I am not tempted by such lifestyles. I am not tempted to pray the song Janis Joplin made famous which pleads for the Lord to buy the singer a Mercedes-Benz.

I am not prepared to pay the price of wealth. I am not willing to give my life to accumulating dollars. I am not prepared to give account for such wealth before God or to my poor neighbors in this hurting world.

Yet I am troubled to know such people. Why? Because to know them is to be tempted. I am not necessarily tempted to envy their wealth. But I *am* tempted to say, "I am not like them. I am not wealthy. Poor me. I am not rich. God's words about affluence and wealth do not apply to me. Since I will never be as rich as them, I need not heed God's warnings about wealth." When I look at the extravagantly wealthy, I forget to look my own suffering neighbor in the eye.

In the insulation of North American lifestyles, many of us do not face the reality of suffering, pain, and hunger. Three decades ago, Michael Harrington pointed out in *The Other America* that we do not see the poor; they are invisible. Instead, we voyeuristically watch "Lifestyles of the Rich and Famous" and compare ourselves to those who have more.[1]

Yet North Americans have the most affluent lifestyles in the world. In the eyes of most of the world, we North Americans are filthy rich. For that reason, it is difficult for us to pray this petition honestly: "Give us this day our daily bread."

The Prayer of the Poor

If I want to contemplate this petition and to be honest about my wealth and poverty, I can remember Frere (Brother) Arnaud. Frere Arnaud lives in the northeast mountains of Haiti, the Western Hemisphere's poorest nation. He is a devout leader of the local Protestant church. When I visited him in 1986, he was feeling discouraged. We sat in the shade of a branch shelter he had erected behind his mud hut. The women were patiently cooking a meal outside.

Frere Arnaud was despondent because his teeth were hurting, as they had for years. He could not afford the seventy-five dollars he needed to have his teeth fixed. That extravagant amount of money equalled several months wages.

If I want to contemplate honestly this petition and *my* wealth, I can reflect on an elderly woman I heard about. She lived in a garbage dump in South Africa. She was happy when white people had parties because they inevitably threw away a lot of "good garbage."

I can also consider a friend in Chicago who was raising a dozen children and grandchildren. Her children were all tempted by gangs and drugs. They all struggled with school. And several became parents when they themselves were still only teenage children. She often told me that God always cared for her and never let her down.

Also in Chicago, I knew an elderly grandmother with many health problems. She could speak no English and single-handedly cared for her little granddaughter. She liked our church because we did not look down on her. She told me God always upheld her.

There was an elderly woman only a few steps from becoming a bag lady. She lived in an inadequate apartment and cared for her ailing and failing parents. Every Sunday, she walked the several miles to church, even in bitter cold and blistering heat. To this day, when I visit Chicago she invariably greets me with a warm hug and a loving kiss.

This petition, "give us this day our daily bread," is important for the poor; it is a prayer of the poor. It is not merely about this life. William A. Dyrness notes that African interpreters see this petition as having eternal implications. African theologian Cyril Okorocha, says, "It is difficult to look forward to a blessed hereafter unless there has been a tangible 'down payment' of that tomorrow in the here and now."[2]

This affects his interpretation of this chapter's petition. "Give us already today, some of tomorrow's bread," he paraphrases. "The concrete provision of needs now becomes, for children of the heavenly Father, a symbol of the future that will be completely manifest at Christ's return."[3]

To pray "give us this day our daily bread" is difficult for most North Americans. Most of us do not worry about daily bread. My freezer is full of bread I bought on sale. (There are plenty of other goodies there as well.) Most of us are far beyond worrying about daily bread. Most people I know are on the road to a "good life" dominated by money, possessions, and material affluence.

When Jesus taught this prayer, he addressed people who knew what it meant to be hungry. They had seen and felt it. Ironically, we know more facts and statistics *about* hunger than those people did. We know about starving countries. We have seen the images on television and in the newspapers. But few of us have been touched by hunger and starvation, although some of our parents have. My parents and grandparents lived through a Netherlands wracked by the Depression and World War II. But I have never known physical want.

Yet my generation is not content. Most of us do not conclude,

"Hey, we are already living better than our parents! Enough is enough." Instead, we keep wanting more and more.

That is not the way of biblical wisdom. One man writes,

> A couple of years ago, I spent a day with my father-in-law, a Kansas farmer, hoisting hay bales from baler to flatbed truck. Afterward, we philosophized about city life and farm life.
>
> "The biggest difference I see," he said, "is that city people tend to expect each year to be better than the last. If they haven't gotten a raise, acquired something new, or find themselves somehow better off, they're dissatisfied.
>
> "On the farm, you don't expect the fields to yield more each year. You expect good years and bad. You can't control the weather, and you pray that you avoid disaster. You work hard and accept what comes."[4]

That Kansas farmer understood that being content with enough is wiser and more sensible than always hoping for more, more, more.

Praying About Bread

Many commentators are surprised that Jesus could pray in such a down-to-earth way. They are astonished that Jesus moves so quickly from the glories of God's name, the marvels of his kingdom, the wonders of his will—to something as crumbly, crummy, and mold-prone as bread.

But other commentators are not bothered by this development. "God wants us to be concerned not only with his affairs, his kingdom, his will, and his name, but also with human affairs, human needs, human hunger."[5] The Lord's Prayer shifts its lens and now directs its focused gaze on human needs. We have quite naturally moved from praise of God and his purposes to intercession and petition on behalf of humanity.

Elsewhere Jesus told the tempter, "One does not live by bread alone, but by every word that comes from the mouth of God" (Matt. 4:4). We cannot live by bread alone, but we cannot live without it either.

And woe, woe to the rich Christian with plenty of bread who tries to tell a person one cannot live by bread alone. "No matter how high the spirit soars . . . the human being will always be dependent on a piece of bread, a cup of water—in short, a handful of matter."[6]

Bread was a staple in Jesus' society. People ate it with virtually every meal. It was the equivalent of rice in Asia or tortillas in Latin America. Others could legitimately pray, "Give us this day our daily rice" or "Give us this day our daily tortillas." In this prayer, *bread* is not just about the loaves that bakers make. It symbolizes all human food (Prov. 20:13) and indeed all the material things we need to survive.

Bread is, of course, also a heavily laden symbol. It is sometimes a nickname for money. But it has many other meanings as well. "Bread is holy because it is associated with the mystery of life, which is sacrosanct."[7] Thus Jesus called himself "living bread" and "bread of life." He fed the multitudes with bread. And thus bread has become one of the elements of communion. Perhaps this petition is one reason many devout Roman Catholics go to daily Mass.

Scholars debate the meaning of the word our Bibles usually translate as *daily*, as in "*daily* bread." This word is not found anywhere else in the Bible or in Greek literature. I accept the arguments that it simply means *sufficient* or *enough*: "Give us this day sufficient or enough bread."

Notice that we pray for enough and sufficient bread. We do not pray for more than we need. We do not pray for a freezer full. We do not pray for extra bread. When God gave daily bread, manna, to the people in the wilderness, he gave them enough for each day. "Gather as much of as each of you needs . . ." (Exod. 16:16). When some tried to gather and hoard extra manna, it was rotten by the next day.

Our society has abundant bread. You may remember the story of Joseph. Egypt had seven years of fabulous affluence. Joseph warned them not to live extravagantly, not to get fat. He cautioned them to use the abundance for the years of hunger. I wonder how long North Americans will continue to live in years of affluence. How long will we get fat on abundance and flesh pots? How long can we close our ears to the hungry, the ones whose years are years of hardship? How long, O Lord, how long?

This verse of the Lord's Prayer says at least two very specific things to North Americans. First, it teaches us to be content and satisfied. Second, it commends the sharing of bread with each other.

Learning That Enough Is Enough

This petition in the Lord's Prayer echoes the wise prayer found in Proverbs 30:8-9:

> Give me neither poverty nor riches;
> feed me with the food that I need,
> or I shall be full, and deny you,
> and say, "Who is the Lord?"
> or I shall be poor, and steal,
> and profane the name of my God.

That author knew that wealth is a barrier to God, a temptation to abandon the faith. Perhaps that is why North America, the wealthiest society in the history of the world, is also such a secular society. We need to learn how to pray, "Feed me with the food that I need." No more and no less. (The author of the Proverbs also indicated that poverty harms the soul.)

This prayer reminds us that God gives us the food. Whether parents provide it, whether we grow it by the sweat of our brow, whether we buy it with money earned from our work, it is ultimately God who gives us the bread. (And woe, woe, to the persons or institutions or economic systems that keep people hungry. They stand between the God-given gift of food and God's intended recipients!)

We ask God for bread, we never own it. No matter how we have come by the bread, we should be thankful, mindful, and content.

> I have learned to be content with whatever I have. I know what it is to have little, and I know what it is to have plenty. In any and all circumstances I have learned the secret of being well-fed and of going hungry, of having plenty and of being in need. (Phil. 4:11b-12)

Our society is far from Paul's spirit. We never have enough. Attending the Detroit Blues Festival proved to be a study of human nature. I enjoyed evenings of blues music. But the music was rudely interrupted by representatives of a potato chips company. They carried huge boxes filled with bags of chips. They tossed the bags randomly into the crowd; people went crazy. They were delighted to grab free bags of potato chips. Some managed to snag four bags. I watched people move to the front with anxious expressions on their face. If they returned to their seats with a potato chip trophy, they smiled happily.

Some vendors sold beer in huge, cheap-looking, gaudy, plastic souvenir beer mugs. Here again, I saw people's urge to amass. Many walked around with empty cups, stacked five, six, or seven high. Carrying these mugs in a crowd was awkward. But there was a purpose: the owners showed off their possessions and visibly boasted about the amount of beer they could drink. Does *our* grabbing consumerism look just as silly from God's perspective?

When we pray for bread, we pray for our needs, not our wants. We do not pray for anymore than we need. On my bulletin board, I have some pictures I clipped from a newspaper in New Orleans. They show an old African-American man caring for his urban garden.

> Gardener Angelo T. Arnona . . . surveys his vegetable patch that grows in the shadows of the New Orleans Towers retirement community, where he lives in Algiers. Arnona, 80, has cultivated the garden in the same lot for five years. What portion of the harvest he doesn't use, he sells to his neighbors and friends in the Towers.

My favorite picture shows a hand-lettered sign that stands in his garden. "Thank you, Jesus, for giving me the strength to make a small garden."[8]

This contented and simple old man reminds me of a Bible-quoting hobo I once read about. He loved to eat catfish that he could catch himself. But he decided to forego this pleasure as he would need first a knife, then a frying pan. He preferred to keep life simple and not accumulate any possessions. He understood that the more we accumulate, the more we are compelled to accumulate.[9] The cycle is endless.

It is far better to learn how to be content. Gregory of Nyssa said in the fourth century,

> So we say to God: Give us bread. Not delicacies or riches, nor magnificent purple robes, golden ornaments or precious stones or silver dishes. Nor do we ask him for landed estates, or military commands, or political leadership. We pray neither for herds of horses and oxen or other cattle in great numbers, nor for a host of slaves. We do not say, give us a prominent position in assemblies of monuments and statues raised to us, nor silken robes and musicians at meals, nor any other thing by which the soul is estranged from the thought of God and higher things; no—but only bread![10]

Pass the Bread

Our city of Windsor is Canada's largest border city and a major point of entry for newcomers, immigrants, and refugees from all over the world. Our congregation is often called on to respond to the dire needs of refugees. At one point or another my work has connected me with newcomers from Rwanda, Vietnam, Honduras, El Salvador, Guatemala, and Mexico.

One cold Sunday morning I needed to drop in on Juan, a Central American refugee who was affiliating with our church. While the winter air was biting and bitter, I saw the apartment's street door was standing wide open. In fact, there was no lock or even a doorknob. In mystery novels, open doors are always signs of looming troubles.

I went up the stairs and found that the apartment door upstairs did not have a lock either. It too stood open. I entered the dark, dirty kitchen. Greasy dishes were piled in the sink. Empty beer bottles littered the floor. The whole place reeked. The carpet had years of grime ground into it.

A small cramped apartment had been converted into a rooming house. Each bedroom door had a lock on it. For the privilege of staying in this room, each person paid $225 per month. This purchased a bedroom and the right to share the aforementioned kitchen and a bathroom I will not describe. (It was worse than the kitchen.) The landlord was reinvesting little of his income in the apartment.

One of the great shocks of my life has been to see the places many refugees end up living in. I encountered atrocious slums in Chicago, but I did not expect to see similar injustices in Canada. This is the blunt end of our economic system which is always quick to exploit the vulnerable and hard-pressed.

Unfortunately, many refugees in Windsor live in similar or worse conditions. One single mother lived in a small apartment that fronted on an alley. It had no rear exit. The garbage was piled near her door and windows. All night long, strangers would come by and bang on the windows, asking, "When is your husband getting home?" She was terrified.

One thing that particularly disturbed me about Juan's apartment was that it was next door to a huge cathedral. A renowned institution within our city, it had recently spent millions of dollars on renovations.

I wondered whether the parishioners knew their next door neighbors were living in abject poverty. Would they even care? A liturgical congregation, it prays the Lord's Prayer in every service. Did they ever wonder about the implications of praying for "our daily bread"?

The Lord's Prayer teaches us more than the importance of being content. This great prayer shifts on its axis with the phrase "on earth as in heaven." First we gazed toward God. Now we focus on earth (just as God lovingly gazes at earth). God directs our gaze to earth and material needs, toward others.

Thus we do not pray for *my* bread. Rather, we pray for *us* and for *our* bread. "God does not hear the prayer that asks only for *my* bread."[11] When we pray this prayer, we pray collectively for *us* and for *others*. Such a prayer especially includes the hungry. "The plea for bread is correctly prayed only when it is spoken as a plea that we be given food in order that we might give food to others or be strengthened to help others."[12]

As we pray this prayer, God calls us to listen to the cries of the hungry and starving, the cries that he hears in heaven. In the fourth century, St. Basil the Great said:

> The bread that is spoiling in your house belongs to the hungry. The shoes that are mildewing under your bed belong to those who have none. The clothes stored away in your trunk belong to those

> who are naked. The money that depreciates in your treasury belongs to the poor![13]

Prayer is a crucial way of coping with the difficulty of living as citizens of heaven while on earth. This prayer reminds us that the kingdom is not complete when there are hungry people.

True prayer always points to pain and need. The greatest Christians are those who can face pain and bring healing, those who can find meaning even in the face of crucifixion. The world sensationalizes pain and insulates us from it, as if pain is contagious. We avoid and isolate the starving poor, just as Jesus' society used to cut off lepers.

But the Lord's Prayer points to the places of our deepest hurts, wounds, weaknesses, and brokenness. This petition calls us to be compassionately mindful of the hunger of others. When we pray "give us this day our daily bread," we are called to act, to consume less, to live simply. We are to share, to feed the hungry, to work for justice. Isaiah 58 rhetorically asks what God wants.

> Is it not to share your bread with the hungry,
> and bring the homeless poor into your house;
> when you see the naked, to cover them,
> and not to hide yourself from your own kin?
> Then your light shall break forth like the dawn,
> and your healing shall spring up quickly. (Isa. 58:7-8)

As Jesus taught long ago in the incident of the widow's mite, it is the poor who can best teach us about generosity, giving, and sharing. Deborah Kay Bragg writes, "It was during the six months I spent in Nicaragua during my junior year at college that I learned how to trust God for daily bread." She lived in a village wracked by both droughts and floods. To top it off, the corn harvest was almost ruined by an insect infestation. Because the ports were mined, insecticide could not be obtained.

One morning, Bragg was awakened early by her "mother," the woman who was hosting Bragg. They needed to harvest as much corn as possible, before the insects got it all. It was a twenty-minute hike.

> The field looked as if a fire had swept through it. Black worms hung greedily on bare stalks, swaying heavily in the wind.

> My mother got on her hands and knees and began praying to God, pleading with God to help her husband accept the fact that all his hard work was in vain and that he would not be able to provide for his family. Then she praised God for the corn she would be able to get that day—and thanked God for teaching all in the community a lesson on trusting the Lord for food and the future.
>
> I had never seen anyone pray to God in the middle of a field, on bended knees, with a corn stalk in her hand. I didn't know what to think. But after her words sank into my heart, I realized that this was the food God had decided to give us for the next few months, and I fell to my knees. Together we thanked God for God's love and kindness.

The women worked long and hard together, managing to collect two large bags filled with corn ears. Putting their bags on their heads, they began to walk back. When they met anyone friendly, Bragg's mother gave them a skirtful of corn. Bragg was surprised by this. Soon her mother had almost no food left. Then they stopped at a home for water.

> We drank, and my mother gave the woman enough corn for her entire family—out of my bag! I had picked that corn. It was mine!
>
> The resentment stayed with me as we roasted the corn over the fire. Because of my mother's generosity with my corn and hers, we had only two ears each, and that was our breakfast and lunch.

Bragg was unable to get over her feelings of anxious resentment. Then a miracle happened. A "mother and her daughters, on their way back from their field, stopped by our house and left enough corn with my mother to feed all of us. This sharing kept us going my whole stay!"[14]

Many North Americans with overseas experiences of poverty can share similar stories. Sister Theresa McSheffrey was traveling by bus one night in Tanzania. In an accident, the bus overturned. The next morning, the passengers began to share their food with one another.

> When a woman gave her last piece of bread to Theresa, the missioner responded, "Mama, save that for yourself and your little girl." The woman smiled and replied, "Sister, we have some bread now, and we all share that. If we have nothing to eat later, we will share the hunger."[15]

11

Forgive Us Our Trespasses, Sins, and Debts

"Forgive us our debts" (Matthew: RSV, NRSV, NIV, KJV, JB)
"Forgive us the wrong we have done" (Matthew: NEB)
"Forgive us our sins" (Luke: RSV, NRSV, NIV, KJV, NEB, NAB, JB)

The Gift of Our Dependence

With this petition, "forgive us our debts," the Lord's Prayer continues what was begun in the last petition about bread. The prayer continues to concern itself with basic human needs. Daily bread refers to our basic material needs. Now we ask for something we need in all of our relationships. One authoritative commentator on the Lord's Prayer even finds it significant that this petition begins with the word *and*.

> The petition is linked with the . . . one for bread by a simple "and." The same poverty and need which there oppress a [person's] body here plague [one's] heart. Just as [one's] body cannot live without the bread that God gives [one] today, so too [one's] heart cannot live without the forgiveness that God alone can give. The same grace that restores [one's] body raises [one's] heart; just as a [person] experiences the . . . grace of God in eating and drinking, so too in forgiveness [one] experiences the same . . . grace which makes [one] a child in [the] Father's house and frees [one] from debt and failure.[1]

It is no surprise that the Lord's Prayer is regularly prayed at Alcoholics Anonymous (AA) meetings. Although AA is not an explicitly Christian organization, it has adopted our primary prayer. AA members recognize their vulnerability and their need for God. This is also a central implication of our Lord's Prayer. AA calls people to live day by day, "one day at a time." The Lord's Prayer calls us to pray for our daily bread, sufficient for today's need. At AA, you are likely to be asked if you made it *today*. "Are you sober today—just for today?"[2]

I know of a number of alcoholic Christians involved with AA. Several are *not* involved with a local church. Some Christians say the local church is particularly bad at dealing with issues of dependency and vulnerability.

> "None of us can make it on our own—isn't that why Jesus came?" he explained. "Yet most church people give off a self-satisfied air of piety or superiority. I don't sense them consciously leaning on God or each other. Their lives appear to be in order. An alcoholic who goes to church feels inferior and incomplete." He sat in silence for a while, until a smile began to crease his face. "It's a funny thing," he said at last. "What I hate most about myself, my alcoholism, was the one thing God used to bring me back to him. Because of it, I know I can't survive without him. Maybe that's the redeeming value of alcoholics. Maybe God is calling us alcoholics to teach the saints what it means to be dependent on him and on his community on earth."[3]

We are dependent on God. We are vulnerable before God. We owe God debts. We can never succeed on our own. Our dependent vulnerability is not a law, a must, an ought, a should, or a have-to. Our dependent vulnerability is a *fact*.

In the face of that fact, our Lord's Prayer reminds us that we *can* rely on God, that we *may* count on God, that we are *free* to look to God. Our dependent vulnerability is not merely a painful reality. It is a wonderful privilege.

Debts, Sins, or Trespasses?

Once again, Matthew and Luke present these petitions in slightly different ways.

> And forgive us our *debts*, as we also have forgiven our *debtors*. (Matt. 6:12)
> And forgive us our *sins*, for we ourselves forgive everyone *indebted* to us. (Luke 11:4a)

Matthew talks about *debts*. Luke talks about *sins*. Both talk about debtors or those who are indebted. Luke's word *sin* sounds more theological to us. Many scholars believe that Luke's Lord's Prayer is usually closest to the original version. But here they believe Matthew's prayer is more accurate. *Debts* is an Aramaic word and thus more likely the word originally used by Jesus.

A third word comes into play here. We usually do not pray either Matthew's or Luke's version. The most common version of this petition is "and forgive us our *trespasses* as we forgive those who *trespass* against us." That version has a long historical tradition and precedent but is not found in the Bible itself. The word *trespass* is found, however, in Matthew 6:14-15 where it is explicitly linked to our Lord's Prayer.

This is the longest, most complex petition in the Lord's Prayer. It comes in two parts. First, it asks God to do something *for* us, "forgive us our debts/sins." Then it promises that we will *do* something ourselves. In this chapter, we focus only on the first half of the petition.

The Good News and the Bad News

The petition "forgive us our debts" reminds us of two important truths. One is good news and the other bad news. First the bad news. This petition reminds of our sinfulness. By now some of us are tired of this subject. But the biblical testimony is clear. We are all sinners. Three different New Testament authors tell this important truth in three different ways.

> All have sinned and fall short of the glory of God. (Rom. 3:23)
> All of us make many mistakes. (James 3:2a)
> If we say that we have no sin, we deceive ourselves, and the truth is not in us. (1 John 1:8)

At the beginning of this chapter, we reflected on lessons AA teaches. A Christian we referred to then says alcoholics can often deal better with their alcoholism in AA than they can in church! Some alcoholics explain their resistance to church

> by recounting stories of rejection, judgment, "a guilt trip." A local church is the last place they would stand up and declare, "Hi, I'm Tom. I'm an alcoholic and a drug addict." No one would holler back "Hi, Tom!"[4]

Thus a Christian alcoholic told Philip Yancey it was AA—not the church—which helped him understand and accept the notion of original sin. His alcoholism convinced him of sin's reality.

> In fact, although many Christians balk at the doctrine, original sin makes perfect sense to the average AA person. We express that truth every time we introduce ourselves: "I'm Tom. I'm an alcoholic." No one ever gets away with saying "I *was* an alcoholic."[5]

The second and more important truth of this petition is the good news of the forgiving mercy of God. God is infinitely merciful to us. The unlimited mercy of God is, of course, reflected in the ministry, death, and resurrection of Jesus. Given the bad news of our own sinfulness, it is good news to know that God's loving mercy outweighs our own evil.

Thus we do not rely on God because we are so good, but in fact because we are so in need of God. Morton Kelsey says, "The church is not a museum for saints but a hospital for sinners."[6] Just as we all have sin and brokenness in common, we also all have God's grace in common. It is a gift that unites us all.

When my daughter was four, she learned the ritual of Eeny Meeny Miney Moe. This helped her make hard decisions. She also used it to decide who could do something first. More and more, it was the determining factor in her allocation of privileges. No mental slouch, she soon figured out how to make Eeny Meeny Miney Moe come out according to her plan.

One day she went through the Eeny Meeny Miney Moe routine simply for the joy of rhyming repetition. At the end of the verse, she danced and crowed, "I'm Moe! I'm Moe! I'm Moe!"

Our two-year old son also wanted to be a Moe. (Of him, we often say, "Monkey see, monkey *too*.") He mimicked her. An argument quickly ensued, both claiming, "I'm Moe!"

Fortunately, we parents did not need to intervene. In Solomonic wisdom, Erin did an Eeny Meeny Miney Moe recount. (Remember, she had figured out how to manipulate this system.) Lo and behold, Paul was now a Moe too! So the two Moes commenced to dance happily: "I'm Moe!" "I'm Moe!"

God's grace has precisely the same dynamic. In spite of our sin, God forgives and *recounts* so as to extend his grace in a gift of mercy that embraces us all.

Indebted to God

There are two ways of being indebted to God. First, we cannot begin to give back to God all the gifts and graces he offers. These are often regarded as debts of gratitude. Karl Barth says,

> We are God's debtors. We owe him not something, whether it be little or much, but quite simply . . . we owe him ourselves, since we are his creatures, sustained and nourished by his goodness. We, his children, called by his word, admitted to the service of his glorification—we, brothers and sisters of the man Jesus Christ—come short of what we owe to God.[7]

The second kind of indebtedness is caused by our sin before God. We fail God. We violate our relationship with him. We go astray. The main theme of the Bible is God's patient, longsuffering, and forgiving love. Sometimes we think that forgiveness is a theme new to the New Testament. But forgiveness already works its way throughout the Old Testament too.

> The Lord is merciful and gracious,
>   slow to anger and abounding in steadfast love.
> He will not always accuse,
>   nor will he keep his anger forever.
> He does not deal with us according to our sins,
>   nor repay us according to our iniquities.
> For as the heavens are high above the earth,
>   so great is his steadfast love
>   toward those who fear him;
> as far as the east is from the west,
>   so far he removes our transgressions from us.
> As a father has compassion for his children
>   so the Lord has compassion for those who fear him.
> (Ps. 103:8-13)

God's forgiving far outweighs, outruns, outlasts any interest he may have in revenge, punishment, retaliation, and retribution. "Mercy triumphs over judgment" (James 2:13b). Thus Jesus forgave those who killed him: "Father, forgive them; for they do not know what they are doing" (Luke 23:34a).

Similarly, as he envisioned Jesus even while being murdered, Stephen the first martyr forgave his assassins: "Lord, do not hold this sin against them" (Acts 7:60b).

The story is told that a nun had a vision of Christ. When she told her bishop, he demanded she prove the validity of her vision. According to him, she could verify this by asking Christ about the bishop's most recent sin.

"If you can answer that question," said the bishop, "then I will know your vision is true."

Some time later, she reported to the bishop that she had another vision.

"Very well," responded the bishop, "what did Christ say was my most recent sin?"

The nun reported that Jesus said, "I don't remember." The bishop felt this proved the nun was telling the truth.[8]

Forgiveness means release. When we hold something against someone, or hold something over them, forgiveness frees them from those bonds. We will see in our next chapter how difficult it sometimes is to forgive. However, sometimes *asking* for forgiveness is just as difficult as offering forgiveness. It is hard to admit that we need forgiveness. We hang back from God's mercy, we hesitate, we keep things in reserve. The psalmist discusses the painful consequences of his refusal to confess his sins to God.

> While I kept silence, my body wasted away
>   through groaning all day long.
> For day and night your hand was heavy upon me;
>   my strength was dried up as by the heat of summer.
> (Ps. 32:3-4)

There have been times when Christians prayed the whole Lord's Prayer but omitted this one petition! In the fifth century, a certain heresy said that Christians could become so good they might no longer needed to pray the petition.[9] The church took over a century to refute this idea.

But even when we confess our sins, we do not always believe forgiveness is accomplished. Once our daughter took off on her bike, riding around the block with her friends. In the process, they crossed a street and moved out of our view. The rule in our household at the time was that she could only ride where we could see her from the house. Lorna found out about Erin's transgression—as mothers are wont to do—and the two of them sorted the difficulty out.

But that night at supper, the four of us were talking about various things when Erin suddenly looked stricken.

"What's wrong, Erin?" we asked several times.

Finally she said, "I just thought of something I did today, but I don't want to tell Papa."

"Well, tell us, Erin."

"I don't want to."

"Believe us, Erin. You'll feel better if you talk about it."

This went back and forth several times until Erin told me what had happened. We processed it. She was surprised that telling me did not hurt as badly as she feared. We wanted her to know that talking about problems is better than keeping such things secret.

Later that evening, I took the children to the park. From the back of the car, Erin sadly told me, "I can't stop thinking about what I did today."

"Well, Erin, you told us all about it and we talked about it. We forgave you. It's over now, so we can leave it alone."

"I can't leave it alone," she said.

Erin found it hard to experience the release of forgiveness. Yet shortly thereafter, we even let her ride around the block occasionally.

To pray the Lord's Prayer is to admit that we are sinners. We pray, not as righteous people, but as forgiven sinners. And in the Lord's Prayer we find the consolation of God's forgiveness.

When I was a child, we lived near a forest beside the Welland Canal. I was strictly forbidden to go into the forest or near the canal. As a six-year old, I was one day unable to overcome temptation. Walking home from school, I strolled into the woods. I was wearing a black, woolly coat my mother had made for me. I loved that garment, which I called my "bear coat."

I walked through the woods and along the canal. I was careful. Nothing terrible happened. But as I moved through the bushes, my coat picked up hundreds of burrs.

By the time I got home, I was feeling sick with fear and guilt. I knew I had done wrong. I was never good at lying to my parents. And the burrs on my coat gave away my transgression. I decided to preempt my inevitable punishment by recommending a punishment: I would clean the coat myself. My mother accepted.

I sat in the garage futilely trying to pick all the burrs from my woolly coat. It seemed I was getting nowhere. I do not know how long I sat there, but it felt like hours. Finally my mother came outside and cleaned the coat herself.

All the elements of the gospel are in this story. We transgress against our heavenly parent's best advice. Found out, we are unable to "make good" on our own. So our Father takes responsibility for dealing with our punishment.

John Newton lived during the eighteenth century and eventually became a pastor and the author of great hymns. Among other hymns, he wrote "Glorious Things of Thee Are Spoken." I thought of Newton recently when I saw an exhibit about him in a black-history museum.

Before his conversion, Newton was for many years a cruel slave trader. But after his conversion, he became a pastor and worked for the abolition of slavery. What always astounds me about his story is that he authored "Amazing Grace."

In one of God's divine ironies, a hymn penned by a former slave trader has been particularly adopted by black congregations. In fact, while the lyrics of that hymn are from Newton, the origin of the present tune is unknown. It is possible the tune evolved from African-American folk music that had its roots in Africa. This hymn is a potent symbol of reconciliation.

Newton, the sinner, saw himself accurately when he sung of himself "a wretch like me." But because of his honest self-reckoning, he experienced the depths, heights, and glories of God's great grace.

> The Lord has promised good to me,
> His Word my hope secures;
> He will my shield and portion be,
> As long as life endures.

While I have never had a good grasp of poetry, I am particularly touched and moved by a seventeenth-century poem named "Love," by George Herbert. This poem helped spark the conversion of Simone Weil to Christianity.

> Love bade me welcome; yet my soul drew back
> Guiltie of dust and sinne.
> But quick-ey'd Love, observing me grow slack
> From my first entrance in,
> Drew nearer to me, sweetly questioning,
> If I lack'd any thing.
>
> A guest, I answered, worthy to be here:
> Love said, You shall be he.
> I the unkind, ungrateful? Ah my dear,
> I cannot look on thee.
> Love took my hand, and smiling did reply,
> Who made the eyes but I?
>
> Truth Lord, but I have marr'd them: let my shame
> Go where it doth deserve.
> And know you not, says Love, who bore the blame?
> My dear, then I will serve.
> You must sit down, says Love, and taste my meat:
> So I did sit and eat.[10]

12

As We Forgive Our Debtors

"As we also have forgiven our debtors" (Matthew: RSV, NRSV, NIV)
"As we forgive our debtors" (Matthew: KJV)
"As we have forgiven those who have wronged us" (Matthew: NEB)
"For we ourselves forgive every one indebted to us" (Luke: NRSV)
"For we also forgive everyone who sins against us" (Luke: NIV)
"For we too forgive all who have done us wrong" (Luke: NEB)

Those Who Trespass Against Us

Between the fireworks and gunfire, July 4 was one of the worst nights of the year for trying to sleep in our Chicago neighborhood. One year was even worse than usual. At 11:00 p.m. I was threatened by a local gang member (a "gang banger" as they call themselves). He and his friends partied all night in the alley behind our house. I was unable to sleep for worrying. And the next morning I was supposed to participate in a wedding service!

At 2:30 a.m., I heard noises in our back yard. Going outside, I found my fears confirmed. A gang member, a "Two-One Boy," was in our yard. He was calling out to his friends. I considered ignoring him and just going back to bed. But I was worried that he and his friends might damage our property.

I stepped out where he could see me. "I'm afraid I'm going to have to ask you to leave."

"This is the second time you're messing with me!" he scowled.

"What do you mean?"

I did not understand his response, so I asked him again to go. But he challenged me instead. "Well, it's a question of whether you can drag my ______ off this block."

"I'm really not interested in dragging you anywhere. I just want you to leave."

"Can you make me?"

"No, I'm just asking."

"Well, I'm not leaving."

I paused. I tried to think through my options. The first thing I always think of in such situations is calling the police. But if it's against my faith for me to be a police officer and carry a gun, how can I rely on the police to solve my problems for me? Besides, practically speaking, the police only make gangs angry. I had to live with gangs being on my block at all times, whereas the police only passed by occasionally.

I thought about calling my neighbor. But that too could have unwanted repercussions, possibly making this intruder more belligerent. After all, he would then only have to call his friends—and there were a lot of them nearby!

Then I thought of something sure to irritate a person who had been drinking and partying for hours. I was a little surprised by my idea, but in my eagerness to go back to bed I was willing to try almost anything.

"Well, how about if I get a Bible and read it to you." This earned me an unexpected response. He vehemently began telling me about his king, Satan. He warned me that Satan could beat my King anytime. It was eerie. The lights in the alley were behind him so his face was hidden in the shadows. This shrouded face told me all about what Satan had done and could do. "My king and I stand against everything you stand for," he warned.

This conversation was not making any progress as far as I could see. He was giving me a canned rap about his religion. He was unwilling to listen to my convictions, and he was not dealing with the immediate issue of his trespassing on my property.

So I tried to change the direction of our discussion. "What's your name? My name's Arthur."

He paused and studied me. "Arthur," he responded.

"Yes," I said, thinking he was repeating my name. "But what's your name?"

"I already told you," he growled. "Arthur!"

I was surprised. Sharing the same somewhat unusual name meant we had more in common. Until then I could classify him as all kinds of things I was not—gang member, criminal, drinker. But suddenly I knew I needed to treat him with more respect. We were different, but in God's eyes we were also alike.

We talked for thirty minutes. Arthur calmed down. Nevertheless, when I suggested that his Two-One gang meet for negotiation with our neighbors, he refused. He insisted that negotiation would never happen because negotiation means losing power. He warned me about dire consequences if I bothered him or any gang members. In case I had forgotten, he reminded me that his king Satan had given him the power to do anything, from killing people to moving stars in the sky. But he also taught me the secret Two-One handshake and even invited me to join his gang.

I was happy to crawl into bed at 3:00 a.m. Happy to have one less intruder to contend with. Happy that my yard was my own again. I even fell asleep . . . eventually.

But the encounter unsettled me, especially as I reflected on the Lord's Prayer. The law was on my side, but I knew this fellow was part of an oppressed minority. His small acts of intimidation were the only power he had. "As we forgive those who trespass against us," I prayed. Yet I had erected a $400 fence to keep out trespassers.

Clenched Fists

Some time ago I was visiting a Mennonite church in the community where I grew up. Before the service, I met with Ernest Pries. He is around my parents' age and was my principal in grade seven. He will always be "Mr. Pries" to me, even though he now insists I call him "Ernie." We sat together during the service.

Naturally the children's story had to be about a schoolchild getting into trouble and having to go to the principal's office. I leaned over and whispered to Mr. Pries, reminding him that I too had once been sent to his office for a reprimand.

He was surprised. "Did you deserve it?" he asked.

"Yes," I responded.

"Well, then we're even," he concluded. But he asked what I had done.

"I punched a kid in the head while we were in class."

This surprised him even more. "Was he aggravating you?"

I rehearsed the story for him. And though it was over twenty years ago, I still remember it clearly. If forgiveness equals forgetting, then I have not yet learned to forgive.

To this day, I remember what my enemy Philip did as I was in the office awaiting the principal's verdict. He lurked in the hall just outside the office door, rubbing his jaw as if it was still sore. He grimaced as if in pain, hoping to heighten my punishment and further heap burning coals on my head.

Back then, Philip and I knew more about the escalation of hostilities than about forgiveness. Yet I understand that he is now also a pastor!

This reminds me that there are two ways of approaching those who hurt, harm, threaten, or even unsettle us. We can approach them with the tightly clenched fist of hate. Or we can approach with an open, extended hand of forgiveness and letting go.

Forgiveness raises within us intense feelings. I once wrote an article in our local newspaper about Marietta Jaeger, a Christian who learned to forgive the brutal murderer of her own daughter. This article attracted more response than almost anything I have ever written. One woman I did not know, herself a rape victim, phoned me at the church office and had a long conversation with me about the article. When people learned about Marietta, they were moved, amazed, and awed. Most said they could not have done what she did.

But the article also prompted other feelings. An anonymous hate letter was one response. Obscene and spiteful, it was hand-delivered to my house while our children played outside. The night that I received this letter, I did not sleep well. I tried to understand why this person was so disturbed by what I had written and went to such lengths to express displeasure. Aside from the obscene drawing, the person wrote that I was "just like Jesus: a liar and a fraud." At least the person recognized that forgiveness is at the heart of Jesus' message.

Past and Present Forgiveness

Looking at the various translations of this petition at the beginning of the chapter, we note that Matthew frames this petition in the past "as we also have forgiven our debtors." Meanwhile, Luke translates this petition in the present: "for we ourselves forgive every one indebted to us."

This may seem trivial and unimportant, but Matthew's translation causes some theological problems. It seems to suggest that God's forgiveness is conditional on our previous forgiveness of others, "as we also have forgiven." One can make a biblical case for arguing that God's forgiveness is integrally connected to our forgiveness of others. Translated this way, the petition means, "forgive us now as we previously have forgiven others."

This seems to be reinforced elsewhere in the Sermon on the Mount. "For if you forgive others their trespasses, your heavenly Father will also forgive you; but if you do not forgive others, neither will your Father forgive your trespasses" (Matt. 6:14-15). Jesus says, "Whenever you stand praying, forgive, if you have anything against anyone; so that your Father in heaven may also forgive you your trespasses" (Mark 11:25). In the prayer attributed to St. Francis, we say, "It is in forgiving that we are forgiven."

But this immediately raises many *theological* problems. God's forgiveness is supposed to come to us freely, without condition, not because of anything we do. We are completely unable to *earn* forgiveness by our deeds. This is an important insight we dare not forget.

A further difficulty occurs when we try to *compare* God's forgiveness with our forgiveness—forgive just *as* we forgive. Some read here a request that God's mercy be *as* or *like* or compared to our forgiveness of others. But who could stand up under that? If God were as petty, spiteful, and hateful as we humans are, we would all be in deep trouble.

Joachim Jeremias argues that *as* is not a comparison but an observation about cause and effect. Our forgiveness could never compare with God's. "The 'as' implies a causal effect, . . . the correct translation from the Aramaic must be, 'as we also herewith forgive our debtors.' "[1] Thus praying this prayer reinforces Jesus' command that we forgive others. In some mysterious way, God *needs* us to forgive others.

Buechner puts another twist on this petition.

> Jesus is *not* saying that God's forgiveness is conditional upon our forgiving others. In the first place, forgiveness that's conditional isn't really forgiveness at all, just Fair Warning, and in the second place our unforgivingness is among those things . . . which we need to have God forgive us most. What Jesus apparently is saying is the pride which keeps us from forgiving is the same pride which keeps us from accepting forgiveness, and will God please help us do something about it.[2]

Theological experts expend tremendous energy in their heated discussions about this one little phrase. Does God's forgiveness only come *after* we have forgiven? Can we earn forgiveness? While the issues are important, I also find them a little frustrating. Such arguing can be a way of avoiding the obvious. The whole of the Lord's Prayer is practical. But if we argue too long about it, perhaps we will avoid obeying what is clear.

The Lord's Prayer (like all true prayer) leads to some form of doing or action. It leads to faithfulness: hallowed be thy name, thy kingdom come, thy will be done on earth as in heaven, and give us our daily bread all have practical consequences. One can almost imagine the Lord saying, "Stop all this vain and futile arguing *about* forgiveness. Learn how to forgive and just do it."

No matter how you approach these theological questions, the underlying practical intent cannot be ignored or avoided. If we pray this prayer, we will learn to forgive and we *will* forgive.

Thus Luke's version is especially clear: "For we ourselves forgive every one indebted to us." Forgiving others is the inevitable result of knowing God's forgiveness. "Even if the debts of our offenders appear to us to be very heavy, they are always infinitely lighter than ours with God."[3]

Marietta Jaeger often alludes to the destructive effects she sees coming from lack of forgiveness in the lives of others. She told me, "Unforgiveness undoes us. God is the best psychiatrist going. He knows the only way we're ever going to be whole and healthy and happy is when we know how to forgive."

Even so, we do not forgive merely because it works or does us good. The call to forgiveness is not necessarily practical or realistic. We forgive because God forgave us through Jesus Christ and to be obedient is to be forgiving. We forgive because this faithful imitation is the most appropriate way to show our gratitude to God and indeed to worship God.

The Forgiveness of Debts

In the original Lord's Prayer, the key word was *debts*, not sins. This prayer is a literal request to forgive all debts, including monetary debts. John Howard Yoder argues that

> Jesus is not simply recommending vaguely that we might pardon those who have bothered us or made us trouble, but tells us purely and simply to erase the debts of those who owe us money; which is to say, practice the Jubilee.[4]

Jesus' reference hearkens back to many Old Testament laws. The Israelites, for example, were not permitted to charge interest on their loans. This seems strange to us since our capitalist system is based on the collection of interest. Yet I know many people who are enslaved by payment plans and mortgages.

The poor are often further ensnared in cycles of poverty because of the temptations of credit cards and impulse buying. Those who tempt the weak with credit schemes have much to answer for. On a more important level, many Third World nations find themselves deeply indebted. The interest payments on their loans sometimes exceed their gross national production!

In 1990, George Bush proposed that Congress write off and forgive Egypt's $7-billion military debt to the United States. This forgiveness was not unconditional, but a response to Egypt's support during the early stages of the Persian Gulf crisis. Besides the military debt, Egypt owes $6 billion in nonmilitary loans. That gives us a small glimpse into the magnitude of the indebtedness many countries carry. Often the attempts to pay those monolithic debts impede progress and development.

Besides prohibitions against charging interest, God wanted a sabbath year observed every seven years. During those years God wanted all debts canceled. "And this is the manner of the remission: every creditor shall remit the claim that is held against a neighbor" (Deut. 15:2). People were also expected to make routine loans during the sixth year, even though the chance of repayment was especially slim.

Another relevant law was the Jubilee, scheduled for every fifty years. At that time, lands (whether they had been sold or lost in bankruptcy) were to be returned to their original owners. Jesus is thought to have been referring to the Jubilee when he said that he came "to proclaim the year of the Lord's favor" (Luke 4:19). The Lord's Prayer, the model of Christian prayer, echoes the Jubilee in its petition that God "forgive us our debts, as we forgive our debtors."

This prayer is about real and actual debts, including financial debts. It is not just about sins or offenses. Perhaps this interpretation is new to many. This prayer challenges the very ways our economy is arranged. When Jesus prays about the forgiveness of debts, he reminds us of the year of Jubilee and calls us to an ideal where debts are canceled, the oppressed go free, and the land is given rest.

Jesus is not referring only to what we might consider spiritual debts. He shows us that even monetary debts are spiritual debts, for money is always an issue closely connected to our faith. Money and its use is a spiritual issue.

As a pastor, I once dealt with an emergency involving a runaway teenager. To alleviate a potentially dangerous situation, I needed to put him immediately on a bus to a western province. There he would rejoin his nuclear family. As the teenager appeared to be in some danger from people here in Windsor, there was almost no time to accomplish this. But I did not have the money to pay for the trip.

A church family loaned the money. The professing Christian who received the money promised to pay it back. But we never heard again from this debtor, and I suspect we will probably never hear from him.

Yet we did right. When I raised the matter of the unpaid loan with the church family, they said not to worry about it. "Just forget it. If our kids were ever in trouble, we hope someone would do the same for them," they said. They were acting in the spirit of the Lord's Prayer.

When Jesus was anointed by a sinful woman, the righteous wanted to condemn both Jesus and the woman. Jesus said,

> "A certain creditor had two debtors; one owed five hundred denarii, and the other fifty. When they could not pay, he canceled the debts for both of them. Now which of them will love him more?"
>
> Simon answered, "I suppose the one for whom he canceled the greater debt."
>
> And Jesus said to him, "You have judged rightly." (Luke 7:41-43)

The way we treat those who owe us money also reflects our understanding of God and what he has done for us.

An Astounding Example

Some dismiss Jesus' call to forgiveness as naively idealistic, unrealistically impossible. They ask, "Could you forgive someone who brutally murdered a loved one, say one of your children?"

Most of us cannot answer such questions honestly. But my friend Marietta Jaeger testifies to her own dramatic experience of forgiveness in just such horrible circumstances. Her seven-year-old daughter was kidnapped. For over a year, Marietta did not know where her daughter was. Later she learned the girl had been assaulted and killed. Yet Marietta forgave the murderer.

I asked how God had taught her to forgive. She believes God used the year of waiting for news about her daughter as a way of preparing her heart to learn how to forgive. While waiting, a special priest visited the family.

The priest was originally from Yugoslavia, where he was the oldest of thirteen children. After World War II, the Communists took over his country. Soldiers came to his hometown and called in his father, the mayor, for a special conference. They demanded that the mayor discourage the townspeople from practicing and celebrating religious feasts and holidays. Instead they were to concentrate on state holidays.

The mayor, a devout Roman Catholic, adamantly refused and obstinately continued to attend daily Mass himself. This flagrant disobedience was too much for the authorities. They persuaded a cousin of the priest to betray the mayor by arranging a family gathering. Soldiers raided the gathering and machine gunned the priest's parents and ten of his siblings.

The priest, one of his oldest brothers, and the youngest brother (eleven years old) escaped and went into hiding for six months. But people eventually persuaded the priest that living underground was not healthy for a little boy. They encouraged him to send the boy home to other relatives. Surely he would be able to lead a normal life as the Communists would not bother one so young.

Hesitantly, the priest sent the boy back to his home village. On the day of his return, the little boy went to the cemetery, lit a candle, and prayed for his family. Soldiers stepped out from behind a grotto, shooting and killing the boy.

The priest and his other brother were also separated. The priest was discovered and sent to a concentration camp where he endured torture, including having acid thrown down his throat. He escaped from that camp and got into a refugee camp. From there, he went first to Canada and then to Montana. After some years, he discovered that his brother—the only other survivor—lived in Toledo, Ohio.

The priest eventually felt he could not celebrate his twenty-fifth ordination anniversary without going back to Yugoslavia, finding his cousin who had betrayed the family, and forgiving him. While he had forgiven the cousin in his heart, it was important to express this forgiveness face-to-face. When the priest returned to Yugoslavia, the cousin hid. Yet the priest found him and did express his forgiveness of the man whose betrayal had unleashed a cycle of unimaginable suffering and horror.

Marietta was impressed. She told me,

> God was working on me. I was already feeling a call to be willing to forgive. I could look at this man and see that it was possible. He was a beacon for me, showing that you could have that change of heart and God would be faithful to you.

The Challenge of Reconciliation

A friend of mine is a convert to Anabaptism, a so-called new Mennonite. In high school, he became a Christian but had not yet met any Mennonites. At that time, he was interested in peace issues. He told me it felt "natural" to believe in peace. But as he became involved in a certain church, they encouraged him *away* from a peace stance. Only in later years, when he found the Mennonites, did he find his peace position again. Among Mennonites he could believe what came naturally.

But my friend is an exception. To most, forgiveness, reconciliation, and peacemaking do not feel natural. Most think that hatred, anger, and revenge are natural and normal. The war in the Persian Gulf surrounded the writing of this book. Most seemed to find that violent encounter quite normal.

In Genesis 4, there is a passage about Lamech. He brags to his wives,

> I have killed a man for wounding me,
>   a young man for striking me.
> If Cain is avenged sevenfold,
>   truly Lamech seventy-sevenfold. (Gen. 4:23b-24)

Ironically, this story is found in my Bible under the subtitle "Beginnings of Civilization"! While Lamech boasted about seventy-sevenfold revenge, Jesus said this about how often we are to extend forgiveness: "Not seven times, but, I tell you, seventy-seven times" (Matt. 18:22).

Although forgiveness may be difficult, it is central to our faith. We might think crime victims would find it difficult to forgive, yet forgiveness is a basic need for many. While the press and the politicians often advocate being tougher on crime, victims are not healed through retribution and revenge which do not bring healing. In fact, victims are often more open to alternative and merciful sentences than the general public! Nevertheless, forgiveness can be neither hurried nor forced.

Frederick Buechner has a helpful description of forgiveness.

> To forgive somebody is to say one way or another, "You have done something unspeakable, and by all rights I should call it quits between us. Both my pride and my principles . . . demand no less. However, although I make no guarantee that I will be able to forget what you've done and though we may both carry the scars for life, I refuse to let it stand between us. I still want you for my friend."
>
> To accept forgiveness means to admit that you've done something unspeakable that needs to be forgiven, and thus both parties must swallow the same thing: their pride.[5]

Without forgiveness before God and with each other, we would be trapped in cycles of revenge and anger. We have already seen that our forgiveness before God is intimately connected with our forgiveness of others. "This willingness to forgive is . . . the hand which Jesus' disciples reach out toward God's forgiveness."[6]

Thus Thomas Merton wrote, "When we extend our hand to the enemy, God reaches out to both of us. For it is God first of all who extends our hand to the enemy."[7] Similarly, I have heard that George Herbert said, "He that cannot forgive others, breaks the bridge over which he himself must pass if he would ever reach heaven; for every one has need to be forgiven."

The truth is that hate and the thirst for revenge often give us a peculiarly warped joy, even as it eats us up inside. I remember hearing Garrison Keillor say in one of his stories, "O Lord, forgive that person—but please not right away." But Jesus warns us that forgiveness cannot be clung to with a clenched fist. It must be released with an open hand.

We cannot learn to forgive by ourselves. It is a skill we acquire within the Christian community. In fact, sometimes we are unable to forgive, and at such times the church offers the forgiveness we cannot.

> We need others to remind us of the word of love when fear and hate and the desire for vengeance threaten to overtake us. We need others perhaps even to speak the word of forgiveness for us, when we ourselves are emotionally and spiritually incapable of it. To be asked to forgive, then, does not mean that one is left alone with that. We forgive as members of the body of the forgiving Christ.[8]

The Freedom of Forgiveness

Forgiveness gives us a way out of our traps. Hate, retaliation, and revenge always makes things worse. Letting go in forgiveness often gives the free release people most need.

In counseling married couples, I have often found that one partner will be particularly insecure and clingy while the other needs more space. The reserved one tries to stay at a distance from the insecure one. This only aggravates the situation.

To the insecure partner that distancing feels like rejection. The insecure one will cling all the harder to a partner—which makes the other flee all the more anxiously.

But when one partner can finally ease up and let go, the other feels freer. If the clingy partner can say, "I will give my other partner space," the second partner often becomes more affectionate. Paradoxically, letting go brings the other closer. Psychologists call this being a "non-anxious presence."

I have seen similar dynamics among parents. Mothers often want to bring their children up gently and easily. Fathers tend to be tougher. This is often a source of conflict. The father decides that the mother is too lax, so he becomes tougher. The mother sees the father becoming tougher, and she gets laxer. So the father gets stricter yet. The cycle spirals. One or both need to say, "I will do what I think is right without reacting to the other."

We see this problem when nations throw bigger and bigger threats into arms races and cold wars. It becomes harder and harder for one party to stop or negotiate for peace.

Yet often punishment and retribution only make things worse. Ireland still threatens homosexuals with life imprisonment. How ironic! Those who engage in same-sex love are accused of a crime and their punishment is to be confined for life in a same-sex society!

Once we lived next door to a single mother and her four-year-old daughter Amber. The little girl was a timid but loving child. Her mother would occasionally get drunk and beat her. The mother often grew tired of being cooped up in a small apartment with her child.

When sweet little Amber got into trouble, her punishment was to be grounded and further confined to the apartment. She stayed with her mother at such times, rather than going outside to play. This, of course, made things worse as they both got more and more on each other's nerves. Amber would get into bigger and bigger trouble and consequently be grounded for longer periods of time. There seemed no way out.

Forgiveness frees us from such destructive cycles. In 1944, Karl A. Menninger, gave a talk to some of his colleagues.

> If we can love: this is the touch-stone. . . . . To our patient who cannot love we must say by our actions that we do love him. You can be angry here if you must be; we know you have had cause. We know you have been wronged. We know you are afraid of your anger, your self-punishment—afraid too, that your anger will arouse our anger and that you will be wronged again and disappointed again and rejected again and driven mad once more. But we are not angry—and you won't be, either, after a while. We are your friends; those about you are all friends; you can relax your defenses and your tensions. As you—and we—come to understand your life better, the warmth of love will begin to replace your present anguish—and you will find yourself getting well.[9]

Loving and forgiving is not always easy, but it is always absolutely essential. Many adult children of alcoholics live with deep bitterness and unresolved anger from their childhood. This can often lead to depression and guilt.

Such people need to learn first that it is *appropriate* to feel anger about the offenses against them. It is also appropriate to confront those who have hurt them and to hope for repentance.

True forgiveness cannot happen until these things happen first. Forgiveness does not mean casually ignoring offenses, but confronting and overcoming them.

Erich Honecker was deposed as East Germany's chief of state while the country was undergoing tremendous change. The turmoil in East Germany received a great deal of attention, but an unpopular act of Christian reconciliation went mostly ignored.

Honecker was widely hated by others. After being ousted from his position, he was not allowed to live in his luxury villa. A Lutheran pastor offered to let the homeless Honecker live in the pastor's guest room. The pastor even paid Honecker's expenses. This was especially surprising since Honecker had once persecuted the church.

This move was widely resented. Many people threatened to quit the church (and some did). The pastor received vile phone calls.

Yet he acted in the spirit of Jesus. As Paul writes, "All this is from God, who reconciled us to himself through Christ, and has given us the ministry of reconciliation. . . . So we are ambassadors for Christ, since God is making his appeal through us; we entreat you on behalf of Christ, be reconciled to God" (2 Cor. 5:18, 20).

13

Bring Us Not into Trial

"And lead us not into temptation" (Matthew, Luke: RSV, NIV, KJV)
"And do not bring us to the time of trial" (Matthew, Luke: NRSV)
"And do not bring us to the test" (Matthew, Luke: NEB)
"Do not subject us to the final test" (Matthew, Luke: NAB)
"And do not put us to the test" (Matthew, Luke: JB)

A Problem Petition

This is the last phrase in Luke's version of the Lord's Prayer. It also brings us close to the end of the Lord's Prayer as Matthew records it. As you can see above, there are many different translations of this particular petition. We ask God not to lead, bring, subject, or put us to temptations, trials, or tests. This is the only petition in the Lord's Prayer stated negatively.

This petition raises many problems and questions. People argue about its exact meaning. James 1:13-16 seems to directly contradict this phrase.

> No one, when tempted, should say, "I am being tempted by God"; for God cannot be tempted by evil and he himself tempts no one. But one is tempted by one's own desire, being lured and enticed by it; then, when that desire has conceived, it gives birth to sin, and that sin, when it is fully grown, gives birth to death. Do not be deceived, my beloved.

Some scholars believe that James is deliberately and specifically refuting the Lord's Prayer here. If God does not tempt us, why then do we ask that God not lead us into temptation?

There is at least one other reason this petition is troubling. Adults know life is a trial, a test. The world is full of temptations. How can we truly expect our lives to be free of temptation? Is this a reasonable request?

Temptation in the Bible

The subject of temptation looms large in the Bible.

> We might call the Bible . . . the "Book of Temptations." On its first pages stands the temptation of the first man and woman, and on its last the prophetic descriptions of the great temptation which is "coming on the whole world, to try those who dwell on the earth" (Rev. 3:10). Between this beginning and this end there stretches the history of the people of God and . . . a continuous chain of temptations which begins with Abraham and does not end with Jesus and his disciples; indeed, to speak of a divine history means to speak of the continuous series of temptations which has gone on since the world was created and will go on until it ends.[1]

The Bible repeatedly warns us about the universal presence and opportunity of temptations and sin. God admonishes Cain, "Sin is lurking at the door; its desire is for you, but you must master it" (Gen. 4:7). Similarly, a familiar New Testament verse cautions, "Discipline yourselves, keep alert. Like a roaring lion your adversary the devil prowls around, looking for someone to devour. Resist him, steadfast in your faith" (1 Pet. 5:8-9a).

The Lord's Prayer is realistic. It reminds us that we are human, fallible, prone to sin. We never stop sinning; we never reach the ideals we hope to achieve.

We may be rooted in and molded by the spirituality of our

Lord's Prayer. We may hallow God's name and pray for his will and kingdom to come. We may count on him for all our needs. We may accept that our sins have been forgiven and learn to forgive the sins of others. Even so, we inevitably sin again and again.

After we have pleaded with God to "forgive us our debts," and after our debts have been erased, we still need God's help. It is said that Martin Luther went to bed praying, "Forgive us our debts" and woke praying, "And bring us not into the time of trial." Both petitions remind us of our absolute spiritual dependence on God. Both petitions remind us of our weakness as humans and of our radical need for God. Following God's forgiveness, we ask for God's ongoing help in leading a new life.

Evil and Temptation

Sin is a verifiable reality. I would prefer to believe that most of us are basically good. "If only people were properly trained, correctly taught, they would choose the good." I would like to think this despite the Bible's passion to say otherwise. I would like to think this despite knowing that Jesus' contemporaries, when faced with absolute truth in Jesus himself, rejected him.

But I know there are evil people in the world. I know all people do evil. For I have seen the suffering hunger of the poor and the oppressed. I have seen institutions and the powers-that-be conspire to keep people in need. I have seen people choose over and over to sin, to do evil, to follow the ways of untruth—despite impressive efforts to counsel them otherwise.

But mostly I grow more and more honest about myself. I am ashamed to see my own tendency to sin. I have been a believer since I was a small child. Yet sometimes I think that I have made no progress whatsoever. I know sin is real. And I know that no amount of teaching or instruction will straighten me out. Without God, I am lost, and I recall the words of Jesus: "Apart from me you can do nothing" (John 15:5b). This petition of the Lord's Prayer partly asks help in avoiding the things which lead to evil or sin.

But it can also mean *trial* or *testing,* as we see in the various translations above. *Testing* means when faith or fidelity are put to the test. *Peirasmos,* the Greek word, usually means the testing of faithfulness. Many argue that the Lord's Prayer refers here specifically to the troubles that will come at the end of the world. "Because you have kept my word of patient endurance, I will keep you from the hour of trial that is coming on the whole world to test the inhabitants of the earth" (Rev. 3:10).

No doubt testing refers partly to the troubles at the end of time. And no doubt it also refers to other tests of our faith. But I remain convinced it is also about those things which tempt us to sin. In fact, sin itself is basically a testing of our faithfulness.

> Testing occurs when we are confronted by events or circumstances that open to us the possibility of . . . disobedience. To be faced with a situation in which one must trust or obey God or trust or obey something other than God—that is testing at its most basic.[2]

Some biblical authors teach that testing can make us better. "Blessed is anyone who endures temptation. Such a one has stood the test and will receive the crown of life that the Lord has promised to those who love him" (James 1:12).

Even so, there is no reason to want to be tested. It is perfectly natural to hope to avoid testing, temptation, and trial. Thus, in the hour of his trial, even Jesus prayed that his testing might pass (Mark 14:32-42). This makes sense of asking God to help us avoid testing and temptation.

Facing Temptation

What we do in response to temptation is especially important. Jesus, of course, is the great example. Throughout his ministry, he was faced with many temptations—and overcame them all. First came the temptations in the desert, but he was continually tempted after that as well.

> Although he was a Son, he learned obedience through what he suffered. (Heb. 5:8)
>
> For we do not have a high priest who is unable to sympathize with our weaknesses, but we have one who in every respect has been tested as we are, yet without sin. (Heb. 4:15)

Jesus' example of endurance and his overcoming of temptation help us. "Because he himself was tested by what he suffered, he is able to help those who are being tested (Heb. 2:18). In 1 Corinthians 10:13, we are assured, "No testing has overtaken you that is not common to everyone. God is faithful, and he will not let you be tested beyond your strength, but with the testing he will also provide the way out so that you may be able to endure it."

The Lord's Prayer is eminently practical. If we pray for daily bread, we are still to work for daily bread as we are able. And we are to share our daily bread with others. The Lord's Prayer always has concrete practical consequences. Thus when we ask God for forgiveness, we are to forgive others as well.

Today's petition also has practical consequences. If we ask the Lord to help us through temptation and testing, then he expects us not to expose ourselves to temptation. If we have problems with gambling, we should not be in a casino. If we have problems with materialism, we should not hang out in malls (and perhaps we should not watch television commercials). If we have problems with alcohol, we should not be in bars. If we have problems with sex, then we should not expose ourselves to sexual temptation. That is just common sense.

Sometimes God preserves us from temptation by telling us to *flee*. When Potiphar's wife was tempting Joseph, he finally realized he needed to run. "He left his garment in her hand, and fled and ran outside" (Gen. 39:12). The Amish and the Hutterites choose to live lives that give them only minimal exposure to the temptations of the world. There is much to commend in their lifestyle. Certainly we more worldly Mennonites are not particularly successful at resisting the world's temptations.

But withdrawal sometimes leaves us less able to cope with temptations. When my uncle went to a Christian college, he was surprised at how rowdy some of his peers were. Raised in isolated rural Christian communities, many did not know how to resist the wiles of the world. When they were in college, they really let loose.

It is not enough to completely avoid temptations. As James notes, temptations come from within. Our society, culture, and media are obsessed with agenda that are temptations. They all tell us that sex is the most important experience one can have and that material goods ought to be our main priority.

Observations About Temptation

We often *know* what is right, even though we *feel* differently and do not want to do what is right. At such times, we want to do something that will feel good. It is then especially important to do what we know to be right.

In counseling, I often notice that people are not always in a position to make good decisions about right or wrong. Many of us go through crisis periods in our lives when we ought to avoid major decisions. That is why counselors sometimes check for signs of suicidal behavior. Likewise, those in troubled marriages are particularly prone to affairs.

Temptation has greater power during crisis. Sometimes my greatest hope as a counselor is to help people get through crisis without making tragic decisions. When things are getting out of hand, we are not in a position to make big choices.

Resisting temptation is a matter of discipline, as we saw in 1 Peter 5:8-9. Alcoholics Anonymous has a HALT rule. Members are to avoid being hungry, angry, lonely, or tired. They know that at such times they are especially prone to bad decisions. It is a good rule and one many of us could learn from.

For example, when I do premarital counseling, I often warn people that the supper hour is the time for most household fights and arguments. People are tired from the day's work and furthermore their blood sugar is low. Their ability to cope is diminished. When I first heard this in a seminary counseling class, I immediately knew this to be true from my own firsthand experience. To avoid temptation, we should postpone airing differences or grievances until after supper.

As one who wrestles with depression, melancholy, anger, loneliness, and despair, I need to observe this rule. When I lead a balanced life, spending enough time in prayer, I fare better.

The "L" (avoid loneliness) of the HALT rule also holds true for this petition. We are again reminded that we need each other, cannot get through life on our own, and are not able to be faithful by ourselves. We need the help of others. The Lord's Prayer says not "lead *me* not" but "lead *us* not." In AA, when things get really bad, one has a buddy who can be called in, someone who can help one get through a rough time.

Part of the problem with our anonymous society is that most of us live privately. Even church members often do not really know how others are living or what they are wrestling with. With the loss of a sense of community or neighborliness has come increasing vulnerability (and opportunity) to temptation.

Most of us hesitate to ask others for help. We think we should be perfect, or at least should look pretty good. As a pastor, I often feel this way. We are ashamed to admit we need help. This is reinforced for us when the occasional person does ask for help and others disdainfully say, "They should know better than that." How did you just respond to me when I admitted I have problems with depression, anger, loneliness, and despair? Did this discredit me in your eyes?

When people are in trouble, Paul counsels gentle assistance.

> My friends, if anyone is detected in a transgression, you who have received the Spirit should restore such a one in a spirit of gentleness. Take care that you yourselves are not tempted. Bear one another's burdens, and in this way you will fulfill the law of Christ. (Gal. 6:1-2)

Another consequence of this petition is that we should guard against *being* a temptation for others. We are not only responsible for what we do, but also for what we tempt others to do. Thus Paul says, "It is good not to . . . do anything that makes your brother or sister stumble" (Rom. 14:21). Likewise, we are particularly warned against tempting children or those who are weak and vulnerable. "If any of you put a stumbling block before one of these little ones who believe in me, it would be better for you if a great millstone were hung around your neck and you were thrown into the sea" (Mark 9:42).

Lorna and I closely monitor what our children watch on television. Recently they wanted to see something new. I watched it with them so we could discuss it together. Again I was shocked by the number of commercials during children's programming. Two times in a half hour one of the children pointed at the TV and said, "I want that." To protect them from the temptations of materialism, we will not let them watch too much television.

There are other ways we are responsible for others. Television and newspapers give us the impression that the worst people in the world are drug pushers and prostitutes. My experience of working and living among the urban poor convinces me that many of those drug pushers and prostitutes felt they had no choice. They were unable to work or they were paid too little for their work. What they do is certainly wrong, but society drives (tempts) many into such occupations. The solution is not a war against drugs, as proposed by our governments. Rather the answer lies in changing society into a place where—as Peter Maurin used to say—it is easier to love and do good.

It is often easy to see and name the sins of others. But our own little evils add up and sometimes we are startled by their fruits. How did I ever get here? But usually we are blind to the incremental, gradual accumulation of sin in our own lives. We would rather voyeuristically look at the sins of others.

When I decided to go to Haiti to serve as an international observer during an election, the local media were interested. They wanted to focus on what they considered "colorful" stories about the dangers I might face there. In other words, they wanted to know about the barbarities of others. I wanted to talk about how the evils of our North American lifestyle harm Third World countries. But that, you see, is not news.

Righteous Temptation

In John Steinbeck's novel *In Dubious Battle* (New York: Viking Penguin, 1979), labor organizers work with California workers during the Depression. One young idealist is killed. A coldhearted organizer exploits the death as a tool in his organizing arsenal. With nary a tear shed for a life lost too young and too soon, he uses the tragic death for his own political ends.

Ever since first reading that novel as a teenager, I have been leery of any crusader—religious, political, or otherwise. I am uncomfortable with those who causally take advantage of any or all opportunities to achieve their own purposes. Steinbeck's organizer showed no sensitivity and no self-examination when he manipulated a tragic death for the advancement of his cause. Those who get caught up in the righteousness of their mission often resort to all manner of questionable methods.

Once I relied on a translator when I was working with some poor French-speaking people. My high school French was inadequate for the job I needed to do. Unfortunately, the translator had strong ideological leanings. It was soon apparent to me—even with my limited French—that he was twisting my words and the words of others as he "translated." He was trying to manipulate both parties towards his preferred politics. No doubt he thought his ends justified his means. But the truth was lost in the interest of our translator's political correctness.

I once served on an interfaith panel which interviewed people on social assistance. Our purpose was to listen to and report their concerns, then make recommendations for reforms to the provincial government. We learned a lot from those who gave reports. Intriguingly, most of the social assistance receivers complained about other welfare cheaters. This was a prevalent theme in almost all of the reports. Many people went on and on about this. Yet such reports did not fit our ideological grid. The poor's "hermeneutical prerogative" only counts when their words fit our predetermined ideas.

Later, when my fellow panelists reported what they learned and recorded it for posterity, they did not repeat the allegations of cheating. Those sentiments and perceptions were unilaterally censored by our panel of clergy. They were only smugly mentioned behind closed doors. We could not afford to let the public know everything the poor said. Those poor persons thought we represented them. In fact, we were only using them.

A prominent bishop on our panel publicly stated that listening to the poor was like "standing on holy ground." Meanwhile we privately curtailed the insights of those we claimed to represent.

All dedicated persons face such temptations. In the passion of a cause, it is easy to lose sight of the intrinsic ambiguity of *all* that we do, the fallenness of our involvements. Seldom do we do anything that is completely pure.

In my own life, I feel a palpable sense of relief when I minister in emergency situations. When someone is in the hospital, my duties are straightforward. Then at least I know what I should be doing and when. My priorities are clear. But in most of life's complexities, doing the right thing is not so obvious.

Pastoring in Chicago's inner city, I was frustrated when acquaintances told me we were doing an admirable thing. We worked where we felt called—but did not feel particularly praiseworthy. We were not suffering. We were not hungry like many of our neighbors. Rather we were challenged by the faith of the poor around us. And we knew that we could always escape from that ghetto even though our neighbors never could.

Eventually we moved to Windsor, where poverty is not as blatant. I felt called to this new location, but I admit to some ambivalence. My new situation was easier. Maybe I was just running from Chicago and an ever-increasing possibility of burnout.

On the other hand, remaining in Chicago was a hindrance to the appointment of a Latino pastor in our largely Mexican congregation. After my leaving, that important priority was fulfilled. So my Chicago experience was important although in many ways it was ambiguous. My entire life remains ambiguous—a mixed bag of pure and impure motives.

That's okay with me. I never want to get caught up in the blindered self-righteousness of Steinbeck's organizer. Far better to be a person who scrutinizes oneself. For me, disciplined prayer is an important way of keeping my priorities straight even in the midst of ambiguities. It is a reminder of my permanent fallenness and a call to rely on God's grace, not my own purity.

As we are tempted, let us hang on to God's promises and reassurances. God is faithful. And let us heed Jesus' advice. "Stay awake and pray that you may not come into the time of trial; the spirit indeed is willing but the flesh is weak" (Matt. 26:41).

The psalmist has a prayer that is important to me.

> Search me, O God, and know my heart!
> Test me and know my thoughts!
> See if there is any wicked way in me,
> and lead me in the way everlasting! (Ps. 139:23-24)

14

But Deliver Us from Evil

"But deliver us from evil" (Matthew: RSV, KJV)
"But deliver us from the evil one" (Matthew: NIV, NAB)
"But rescue us from the evil one" (Matthew: NRSV)
"But save us from the evil one" (Matthew: NEB, JB)

Delivered from a Dungeon

A friend of mine had an intense experience of being delivered from evil. Her story is as exciting—and as miraculous—as Daniel's escapades in the lion's den.

Karen Ridd was then a twenty-eight year-old Canadian working with Peace Brigades International (PBI) in El Salvador. PBI is a nonprofit group committed to nonviolent conflict resolution and the protection of human rights.

In El Salvador at the time, the church—Episcopal, Roman Catholic, Mennonite, Baptist, Lutheran—paid a high price for its faith. In November 1989, six Jesuit priests and their housekeepers were killed by government troops. The Roman Catholic archbishop, Rivera y Damas, continually received death threats. Two prominent Protestant clergy, Lutheran bishop Medardo

Gomez and Baptist pastor Edgar Palacios, fled the country. Forty foreign church workers, including some Mennonites, also left. A Baptist church had sixty-three people working in various projects. Now five remain. Canadian Lutheran pastor Brian Rude was expelled from El Salvador after being held for a day.

The Salvadoran government wanted to be free of international witnesses to the mounting repression. Visas were refused. Foreigners who did visit were not permitted in isolated parts of the country. The Air Force even dropped flyers that said, "Be a patriot, kill a foreigner."

Karen Ridd, a United Church pastor's daughter from Winnipeg, was supposed to be a pawn in this governmental campaign. But she managed to win a few gambits of her own. I first met her a few months later when she told me her story.

In November 1989, Ridd worked in a church center for refugees. "And that's where I was Monday, November 20, when we were wakened at twenty to six. Twenty minutes before the dusk-to-dawn shoot-on-sight curfew was lifted. The National Guard had arrived. We weren't entirely surprised. We had seen other raids on church refugee centers. And we had seen, of course, the killings of the six Jesuit priests only four days earlier, assassinated in the night by government forces."

Four foreigners were taken to the Treasury Police. They included Ridd and Colombian PBI volunteer Marcela Rodriguez Dias. Forced onto the floor of a pickup truck, they were hit on the head when they tried to move. At the jail they were blindfolded and handcuffed. The prisoners stood in a hall where people shoved them and again beat them on the head. One man even threatened to slit their throats.

After a six-hour interrogation, her captors wanted to release Ridd. She, however, glimpsed Marcela—the last of the four. Ridd (tall and blond) suspected that Marcela (a short dark-haired, dark-skinned *Latina*) would receive worse treatment. "And she did have a harder time. She was beaten repeatedly with a heavy object. She was threatened with rape and electrocution. I didn't know those details then.

"When I saw her, it wasn't some big courageous decision not to leave her. It was simply seeing that the only thing was to try and save her." She began arguing for Marcela's release. Ridd was persuaded to go to another part of the jail to sign some papers. Once there, she started arguing again.

"What I thought would happen was that they were going to make me leave, just drag me out of there. They had all the power; I was just some little not-quite-ex-prisoner. Instead they were so surprised anyone would refuse to be freed that they didn't know what to do with me."

She walked back into the jail, where she was returned to an interrogation room and blindfolded and handcuffed again.

Her captors mocked her: "Stupid *gringa,* why did you come back? Did you miss us? Do you like us?"

She pointed out that soldiers should understand the importance of camaraderie.

They were silent for a bit and finally responded, "Yeah we do understand."

Then they put her in the hall near Marcela. Their handcuffs were removed and the two women clung to each other.

"Now the most remarkable thing happened. People kept coming to see us, saying things like, 'Where are the two inseparables?' 'Where are the ones I heard about?' or 'Look at them, they're holding hands.' Not with the kind of mockery that had been going on all day. But with respect, admiration, maybe even a bit of awe. I don't think it was for what we had done or for the strength of our friendship. But for the strength of *human* friendship that can surmount what seem insurmountable obstacles.

"I know where I was. That's a torture center. While there, I heard screams of people being tortured. Those people are torturers, and I know I was treated differently because I'm North American. But for me there is that spark of hope. Even in the darkest of dark places there could be a moment of contact, of human warmth and caring."

The women were later released. This dramatically confirmed her faith in nonviolence. "Taking violent structures and breaking them open by changing the rules and creating a new dynamic. They wanted to get rid of us so badly. I had no idea there was such international pressure generated, especially from Canada. President Cristiani, in the middle of a civil war in his backyard, had to take time out to phone the Treasury Police about some Canadian peace worker. And then had to phone *again* because she'd gone back in!"

Victims of Evil

At first glance, we might think the petition "deliver us from evil" or "the evil one" is the same petition as the last chapter's, "do not bring us to the time of trial." Now we are no longer even in the gospel of Luke, since this petition is only found in Matthew's version of our Lord's Prayer. But this petition also contributes new elements to our understanding of spirituality.

When we talk about *temptation* or *times of trial*, we talk about evil we may submit to. "Lead us not into temptation" addresses evil we may choose to be part of. Temptation is the *opportunity* to *do* evil. But evil is not only something we do. Evil is something *done* to us. We may, of course, choose certain evils. (We Christians tend to be unsympathetic and even judgmental when others give into sin and temptation. "It's their fault," we think.) But all of us, to one degree or another, are victims of evil we don't control. Whether or not we are good, holy, or pure. Whether or not we resist all temptation.

Some evil attacks us. It may be through family problems or suffering, or through injustice or violence. Evil is death in all its forms. When attacked by evil, we naturally cry, "How long, O Lord, how long?" (Rev. 6:10, author's paraphrase).

In our society, where life is comfortable, we are sometimes slow to see the evil around us. We are often blind to the evil that we are part of. Many regard our relative comfort as a blessing, even though our affluence is often at the expense of the world's ecology, the well-being of the poor, and the welfare of our souls. We are in trouble when we do not recognize the evil that assaults us, when we do not know we actually need saving.

Evil is difficult to define. We sometimes say evil is anything against God's purposes. This is true, but also vague. We might say evil is the opposite of Paul's recommended values in Philippians 4. Evil is not true but false. It is not honorable but shameful. It is not just but unjust. It is not pure but corrupt. It is not pleasing but repulsive. It is not commendable but to be rejected.

The Reality of the Evil One

Many ancient versions of this prayer talk not only of evil in general but of "the evil one." That is, of course, the devil or Satan, who is the personification of radical and absolute evil. He is a creature with many names—Beelzebub, deceiver, slanderer, accuser, destroyer, tempter, father of lies.

My acquaintances do not speak much about Satan. They are reacting against people who speak too much about Satan. C. S. Lewis, in *The Screwtape Letters,* warned about two extremes.

> There are two equal and opposite errors into which our race can fall about the devils. One is to disbelieve in their existence. The other is to believe and to feel an excessive and unhealthy interest in them.[1]

Most of us can think of examples and situations where people take "an excessive and unhealthy interest" in Satan. I once preached in a congregation where a woman shared that she almost did not make it to church that morning because Satan sabotaged her iron, thus she could not press her dress! But for the most part, people I know are not excessively interested in Satan.

It is part of Canadian culture, for example, to be polite, reserved, pluralistic, and multicultural. So we do not dare speak about Satan or the devil. Such topics are too disquieting and controversial. As discrete humanitarians, we feel it is bad form to admit there is evil in the world or that people can be in the grip of evil. More than that, we are scientific—and Satan cannot be scientifically proven. He sounds too much like a silly superstition or an imaginary character spoofed at Halloween.

But one need only read the daily newspaper to know evil is real. The Bible is clear that there is a force of evil at work in the world. There is a personality or person behind this evil. That person is Satan. We know little about him, but the fruits of his work are everywhere apparent.

Many think that the devil only works on individuals. But the Bible teaches that Satan and his powers and principalities are at work on all institutional levels. Governments and countries are particularly subject to the work and influence of the devil. In New Testament times, believers understood that the Roman Empire was in the grip of Satan. The same is true of all nations.

M. Scott Peck is a famous and respected psychiatrist. His book *People of the Lie*[2] deals with the reality of evil and even of Satan. My impression is that Peck was surprised to discover evil is real. Yet in his work as a psychotherapist he saw clear evil.

One of Peck's horrible stories is about fifteen-year-old Bobby, hospitalized for depression. Bobby's older brother, Stuart, had committed suicide with a .22 caliber rifle some months earlier. At first Bobby did not seem to suffer any adverse consequences. But then his grades deteriorated. Finally he stole a car and crashed it. (It was the first time he had driven an automobile.)

Peck writes about the youth as being a typically awkward-looking teenager. Bobby did not take good care of himself, and his unwashed hair hung over his eyes. Peck tried a number of tactics to get Bobby talking. But nothing worked. Bobby remained uncommunicative. Finally, as a conversation starter and since it was shortly after Christmas, Peck asked Bobby what he had received as a Christmas gift. Bobby was nonresponsive.

Peck pressed harder, asking what Bobby received. At last Bobby said he had received a gun!

> "A gun?" I repeated stupidly.
> "Yes."
> "What kind of gun?" I asked slowly.
> "A twenty-two."
> "A twenty-two pistol?"
> "No, a twenty-two rifle."
> There was a long moment of silence. I felt as if I had lost my bearings. I wanted to stop the interview. I wanted to go home. Finally I pushed myself to say what had to be said. "I understand that it was with a .22 rifle that your brother killed himself."
> "Yes."[3]

Bobby had not asked for such a gift. In fact, he had asked for a tennis racket. Peck hesitantly continued the conversation.

> "How did you feel, getting the same kind of gun that your brother had?"

"It wasn't the same kind of gun," Bobby replied.

I began to feel better. Maybe I was just confused. "I'm sorry," I said. "I thought they were the same kind of gun."

"It wasn't the same kind of gun," Bobby replied. "It was *the* gun."[4]

Bobby's parents had taken Stuart's suicide weapon and given it to their other son for Christmas. Peck met with these parents the next day and found them hard-working people and faithful churchgoers: "quiet, orderly, solid."[5] The parents were defensive when Peck brought up giving a gun as a Christmas present. The father accused Peck of being a fanatical antigun advocate. The father explained that a gun is "a good present for a boy his age. Most boys his age would give their eyeteeth for a gun."[6]

Peck continued to press the question and the father answered,

> We couldn't afford to get him a new gun. I don't know why you're picking on us. We gave him the best present we could. Money doesn't grow on trees, you know. We're just ordinary working people. We could have sold the gun and made money. But we didn't. We kept it so we could give Bobby a good present."[7]

Of course, it takes little imagination to realize what Bobby must have thought of his present. He saw it as an invitation to go and kill himself too.

Some religious people are too quick to name evil, but many of us are losing the ability to identify and name evil today.

Deliver Us

Given the reality of evil, the "deliver us" is almost a cry of panic. It is the kind of thing we call out when we are in trouble. It is something we might ask of a king, a judge, or someone else who has power over the circumstances of our lives. The Psalms are full of cries for such deliverance. The Greek here very dramatically translates into "snatch us from the jaws."[8]

> Deliver us from evil.
> Save us from evil.
> Snatch us from the jaws of evil.

Rescue us from evil.
Extricate us from evil.

Ultimately, this petition, "deliver us from evil," equals what we usually call *salvation* or *redemption*. To pray "deliver us from evil" is to ask for what Jesus has already accomplished through his death and resurrection. We request something that has been completed. Jesus' death and resurrection assure us that death will not have the last word. Again in the Lord's Prayer we ask for something already promised to us! The petition reminds us where our true security lies.

Note too that this petition includes the word *us*. We are not in this struggle individually, but corporately. Thus as people around the world cry out to God, "Deliver us from evil," that cry challenges us as well. We are called to help and intercede for others. We are called to be advocates for those who are oppressed. Just as "give us this day our daily bread" is a call for us to share bread, so "deliver us from evil" is a call to *share* deliverance (as Karen Ridd *shared* deliverance with Marcela).

But we ourselves do not finally overcome or defeat evil, we only resist it. There are temptations and dangers here. God wins the victories. Ephesians 6 reminds us that our *defenses* against evil are the belt of truth, the breastplate of righteousness, the gospel of peace, the shield of faith, and the word of God.

This petition in the Lord's Prayer realistically recognizes that we will be exposed to evil. We will be victimized by it. But it also reminds us that evil will not have the last word. It claims the promise of the resurrection. In the resurrection we know that death, evil, Satan, and human sin do not have the last word. The resurrection says that even in the midst of evil and trouble God can bring good, life, and peace.

The great hymn "Amazing Grace" talks of being brought through many dangers, toils, and snares. A Chinese word for crisis is *way-chee*. *Way* means "danger," but *chee* means opportunity. A crisis has either possibility—danger or opportunity. The early church experienced two major crises of faith. One centered on the crucifixion of Jesus and the other on Jesus' delayed return. Either crisis could have ended the Jesus movement. But instead both crises renewed and energized the faithful.

The resurrection promises that God's providence works even in the worst times. I know of an auto plant that *remanufactures* cars using mostly recycled parts. Yet it guarantees its cars for up to 100,000 miles. Spending little on new, expensive parts, it invests more in employing people. Even ecological crises can present us with *opportunities* for deliverance from evil.

Delivered from Evil

Most of us know something about oppression, despair, depression, danger, or evil. We know what it is to grieve and mourn, to worry and wonder. At all such times, we do well to pray "deliver us from evil." This prayer reminds us that God has ultimately conquered evil. It reminds us that God loves us and faithfully walks with us. He only asks that we walk with him in return.

Frederick Buechner had an astounding lesson in learning to walk with God. Buechner, a Presbyterian minister, is also a justly acclaimed novelist. Visitors to his home may be surprised to find a rusty, old license plate hanging on a wall in his home.

During one dark period in his life, Buechner was parked beside a road near his home. He was worrying about the uncertain fate of his anorexic teenager. To his surprise, a car suddenly came by. Its vanity plate said T-R-U-S-T.

Buechner reflects, "Of all the words that I needed most to hear, it was trust. It was a chance thing but also a moment of epiphany—revelation—telling me, 'Trust your children, trust yourself, trust God, trust life; just *trust*.' "[9]

Some time later, Buechner was discussing these very anxieties with one of his daughters. Just as they were talking, someone came to the front door. Buechner's daughter answered the door, and he heard a strange male voice. It happened to be the owner of the license plate. The owner (the trust officer in a bank) had heard Buechner preach on the T-R-U-S-T license plate. So the banker decided to give it to Buechner.

To pray "deliver us from evil" is a confession of our ultimate trust in God and the power of Jesus' resurrection.

15

For Thine Is the Kingdom, the Power, and the Glory For Ever

"For thine is the kingdom, and the power, and glory, for ever" (Matthew: KJV)

Where Do Doxologies Come From?

We are now near the end of our study of the Lord's Prayer. Here we consider the *doxology*. A doxology gives praise to God. In the Lord's Prayer's traditional doxology we praise God for his kingdom, power, and glory.

Apart from the King James Version of Matthew, this doxology is not actually found in the Bible. Here the KJV is not true to the oldest biblical documents. Nevertheless, it is generally agreed that the when the Lord's Prayer was prayed—even in the earliest days—some kind of doxology was always used. Quite soon, it is believed, a familiar formula developed: "For thine is the kingdom, and the power, and glory, for ever and ever."

No one believes that our Lord's Prayer concluded either with "lead us not into temptation" (Luke) or with "deliver us from evil" (Matthew). Either would be unheard of as the final word or phrase in a Jewish prayer. At the time, it was usual for a person praying to add a doxology.

The doxology we use is reminiscent of David's doxology in 1 Chronicles 29:11. "Yours, O Lord, are the greatness, the power, the glory, the victory, and the majesty; for all that is in the heavens and on the earth is yours; yours is the kingdom, O Lord, and you are exalted as head above all." Thus this doxology has an ancient tradition and is in the line of Old Testament Judaism.

Understanding the Doxology

The doxology is a fitting conclusion to this prayer. It summarizes the previous petitions. Because of God's kingdom, power, and glory, he is able to give all we have asked for—daily bread, forgiveness of sins, deliverance from both temptation and evil.

The first word in the doxology, "for," means *because*. We pray the Lord's Prayer and make our various requests because of *who* God is. The word "for" reminds us we are permitted and able to pray the Lord's Prayer because of God's character.

The Lord's Prayer begins with praise and worship, "hallowed be thy name." It ends with praise as well, "for thine is the kingdom, the power, and the glory, for ever and ever." We have come full circle. The entire prayer is framed by praise.

Just so our lives and each of our days are to begin and end with praise. "O Lord, our Sovereign, how majestic is your name in all the earth!" (Ps. 8:1). The end of our lives will also bring us to the eternal praise and worship of God. Then, with the elders around the throne, we will sing a doxology that reminds us of the Lord's Prayer. "You are worthy, our Lord and God, to receive glory and honor and power, for you created all things, and by your will they existed and were created" (Rev. 4:11).

There is little need to review here the intent of the word "kingdom"; we have encountered this important idea already in "thy kingdom come." We recall that the kingdom is both present and coming. The kingdom of God is the realm where God's will is done. This doxology, "thine is the kingdom," reminds us that we are to be obedient to God. We owe him our highest loyalty.

The entire doxology reminds us of our place before God. Most of us are too casual about God. As we pray this phrase, we can think back to Psalm 8:4: "What are human beings that you are mindful of them, mortals that you care for them?" The Psalms, the Lord's Prayer, and indeed all Scripture show us God is mindful of us. He does care for us. But that is not something to take for granted or claim to deserve. It is part of his grace.

When prayed with integrity, the Lord's Prayer is like a song that permeates our lives. Sometimes we hear a tune—in church or on the radio—and we cannot get it out of our minds. The harder we try to forget it, the more it permeates our memory. We find ourselves humming it, even when we do not want to!

Strangely enough, it was at an outdoors blues concert that I decided to write a book on the Lord's Prayer. At the concert, I marveled at the glee of the crowd as it danced and swayed to the rhythmic music. Almost no one could sit down or hold still.

But then I noticed one person at the back of the crowd, not moving at all. Dull-eyed and slack-jawed, he was breaking the law by taping the concert. But when I saw his lack of passion, I wondered whether he heard the music as others did. And if he could not appreciate it, why did he bother to tape it? In the same way, why do we bother to pray the Lord's Prayer if we are not prepared to let it challenge and change us at our deepest levels?

We get into trouble when we forget our place before God. Thus we do well to remind ourselves that God has the kingdom, the power, and the glory. We humans are tempted to be arrogant, even self-righteous. We are tempted to play God, like Adam and Eve in the Garden.

For many years, Haiti was ruled by brutal Francois ("Papa Doc") Duvalier. Like all dictators, Duvalier assumed authority and power that belongs to God alone. In 1964, he published a Catechism of the Revolution which ended with a new prayer.

> Our Doc, who are in the National Palace, hallowed be Thy name in the present and future generations. Thy will be done at Port-au-Prince and in the provinces. Give us this day our new Haiti and never forgive the trespasses of the anti-patriots who spit every day on our country. Let them succumb to temptation, and under the weight of their venom, deliver them not from any evil.[1]

The evil of this petition is particularly blatant. Such arrogance leads to unspeakable crimes. Francois Duvalier once said he wanted to kill three hundred opponents a year. But he often killed that many per month.

Duvalier's legacy was continued by his son. President-for-life Jean-Claude Duvalier and his wife, Michèle, single-handedly drove the precarious Haitian economy beyond recovery by their excesses. He favored $250 ties. Their three-million-dollar wedding was listed by the *Guinness Book of World Records* as one of the world's costliest.

When it looked like they would be forced to give up power, Michèle is reported to have said, "If I have to leave, I want to walk in blood from the palace to the airport." Before they left, rumor has it that they had a voodoo priest sacrifice two unbaptized babies—an automatic curse for any successors in the Palace.

Small wonder that the Psalmist longs for God's justice

> so that those from earth
> may strike terror no more! (Ps. 10:18)

John Alexander believes that due reverence before God's kingdom, power, and glory is a solution to human evil.

> I have spent much of my life denouncing oppression and injustice. I do not regret that. But I would like to spend much of the rest of my life increasing people's sense of wonder and majesty, helping myself and others get the scales off our eyes. People with a sense of wonder, those who see the grandeur of the universe, who feel the terrible majesty of God—such people will not participate in oppression. Having once been struck dumb with wonder . . . we will be ignited with horror before evil.[2]

Thine Is the Power

Do we really believe this petition? To whom do we give power? We claim the power is God's, but our governments steal more and more power. Governments claim power to wage war even to preserve rich lifestyles. They tell us they can use our taxes for such evil purposes. They claim the right to take lives. Even as we hear that power corrupts and absolute power corrupts absolutely, we see governments claim ever more power for themselves.

And we also see Christians hungering and even fighting for power in the world. But the Lord's Prayer cautions us. Only God can handle power. Only God is entitled to absolute power.

Jean Vanier is the son of a famous Canadian governor-general. Vanier came from a prestigious family. Yet despite an impressive education and magnificent opportunities, he committed his life to the care of mentally handicapped persons. Like many other prophets, he warns against taking power.

> The greatest seduction is power, whatever type of power . . . even being powerful to do good. The only real answer is to be powerless, so that the power of God can go through us. We must keep always in our mind that to be with the poor is our greatest strength. It seems so little just to be with them yet it's through the littleness that the power of God is manifest. So truth comes daily as we discover the holiness of our [mentally handicapped] people.[3]

Nevertheless, we are tempted to worship the powerful. Thus so-called Christian media celebrate famous Christians—athletes, politicians, movie stars. Power tempts and seduces all of us, even those who think they are doing God's work.

But the gospels point us to the poor and the weak. People like Jean Vanier and Mother Teresa remind us that we are not supposed to be powerful. That is God's job. We best represent God when we listen to his poor and his weak, vulnerable children. Mother Teresa teaches, "We can do no great things; only small things with great love."[4]

> Thus says the Lord: Do not let the wise boast in their wisdom, do not let the mighty boast in their might, do not let the wealthy boast in their wealth; but let those who boast boast in this, that they understand and know me, that I am the Lord; I act with steadfast love, justice, and righteousness in the earth, for in these things I delight, says the Lord. (Jer. 9:23-24)

Our glory is in knowing God and his power. This knowing is different than striving for might. It enables us to live by God's priorities even if they do not appear immediately effective. Martin Luther is said to have once recommended that we work with all our strength as if we could attain perfection, and that we trust with all our strength in God as if all our work was in vain.

And the Glory

As well as giving homage to God's kingdom and authority, this doxology reminds us of God's glory. This we do particularly in attending to God through prayer and worship. We all need to take time to note God's might and works, read the Bible, listen to (and love) our neighbor, and tend God's creation.

By considering the glory of God, we are moved closer to him. By coming near the glory of God, we are enabled in our obedience and strengthened in our resistance to temptations.

> Glory is to God what style is to an artist. A painting by Vermeer, a sonnet by Donne, a Mozart aria—each is so rich with the style of the one who made it that to the connoisseur it couldn't have been made by anybody else, and the effect is staggering. The style of an artist brings us as close to the sound of his voice and the light in his eye as it is possible to get this side of actually shaking hands with him.
>
> In the words of the nineteenth Psalm, "The heavens are telling the glory of God." It is the same thing. To the connoisseur not just sunsets and starry nights but dust storms, rain forests, garter snakes, the human face, are all unmistakably the work of a single hand. Glory is the outward manifestation of that hand in its handiwork. . . . To behold God's glory, to sense his style, is the closest you can get to him this side of Paradise, just as to read King Lear is the closest you can get to Shakespeare.
>
> Glory is what God looks like when for the time being all you have to look at him with is a pair of eyes.[5]

God's glory should inflame our passion to be God's evangelists. Anticipating phrases we find in this doxology, several Psalms make clear that God's glory stirs evangelism.

> All your works shall give thanks to you, O Lord,
> and all your faithful shall bless you.
> They shall speak of the *glory* of your *kingdom,*
> and tell of your *power,*
> to make known to all people your mighty deeds,
> and the glorious splendor of your *kingdom.*

Your *kingdom* is an everlasting *kingdom*,
and your dominion endures throughout all generations. . . .
My mouth will speak the praise of the Lord,
and all flesh will bless his holy name *forever* and *ever*.
(Ps. 145:10-13, 21)

Declare his *glory* among the nations,
his marvelous works among all the peoples. (Ps. 96:3)

As I grow in prayer and learn what it means to pastor others, I increasingly see the need for reverence before God. Dostoevski once noted, "A man who bows down to nothing can never bear the burden of himself." John Alexander compares a mule ride with fear of God.

> Given that a slip could have been a quarter of a mile straight down, that the mules were as uncooperative as mules are said to be, that it was early spring with ice still on the trail, that the Grand Canyon is wondrous. . . . Well, let's just say we developed a serious respect for the Grand Canyon.
>
> Our . . . respect increased when Judy's mule began to munch on a bush three feet below the trail. The mule's back, with Judy on it, pointed at a forty-five degree angle straight toward the bottom. By then, an element of fear was entrenched. . . . mixed with wonder. . . .
>
> The Grand Canyon is not designed for ease of human use but as a display of the grandeur of God and God's creation. It is the kind of place that should strike us dumb and give us a sense of our smallness and creatureliness. The kind of place that can return us to reality after the shallow existence we accept as normal living. . . . The kind of place where you can easily experience joy and peace—and easily get killed.
>
> As a friend said about Canada's Banff National Park: you shouldn't mess with whoever made that.[6]

The Lord's Prayer and its doxology drives us to our knees, the place we began. But it does not leave us kneeling.

> And so, when we have prayed the Lord's Prayer, we rise from our knees and go out to the world and its ways remembering the royal sovereignty of God and pledged to obedience to him, remembering the dynamic power of God and trusting in that power to answer our prayers, remembering the glory of God and living with the reverence which knows that earth is penetrated and permeated with the divine glory.[7]

16

Amen and Amen!

You've Got to Help Me Preach!

The Mennonite congregation nearest to Windsor is in another country. The Peace Community Mennonite Church is in Detroit, Michigan. Although the distance in miles is not great, crossing the borders of our nations and our different church polities do hinder our relationship. But we never regret making the journey to worship, share, and celebrate with sisters and brothers there.

Every October, Peace Community has a special worship service to celebrate the anniversary of Pastor Evelyn Childs' ordination. Actually, Evelyn Childs was ordained in mid-winter, but October weather is better for celebrating!

Our congregation in Windsor is composed of people brought up Mennonite or people who are Mennonite converts. But one looks hard to find Dutch, Swiss or German names in Peace Community Mennonite Church. It is an African-American congregation which worships in an African-American style.

We time-conscious, white, middle-class Canadians are sometimes surprised when worship services there routinely take up to three hours. We are used to our services taking precisely an hour (and the Holy Spirit will just have to fit our schedule).

Once I was feeling a little overwhelmed by the length of a service in Detroit when a visiting speaker there noted, "We don't look at our watches when we are in church. When we go to a baseball game, we are happy if a game goes into overtime. In fact, we get excited. So in church we don't mind whether our service goes into overtime!" I am no baseball fan, but I got the point.

An exciting worship experience came for me when I was invited to preach. My message wasn't what excited me. It was learning, at last, what it was like to preach in an African-American congregation. It was a wondrously affirming experience.

But preaching that sermon also scared and filled me with self-doubt. The opportunity was exciting—but could I do it? Could I connect with people of a different culture and different life experience? Could I keep preaching when people interrupted me?

Well, I consoled myself, it could never be worse than the time I was a seminary student and a guest preacher at a Mennonite church. Midway through my sermon at my most important (and most controversial) point, the whole front row got up and walked out. I knew the parishioners at Peace Community Mennonite had better manners.

As I sat nervously on the podium before my turn to preach, a black Methodist preacher leaned over and whispered into my ear, "Now don't hold back, you hear? Don't be afraid to really preach the gospel. Let the Holy Spirit move!"

Happily, the experience went well. I soon got into the rhythm of making a point, uttering a phrase, then waiting for responses, affirmations, and encouragement. It was a pleasure to say something, then hear "amen," "well," and "ah, yes," ring out. It was a great thing to cite Scripture and immediately be affirmed. My body moved to the congregation's rhythmic responses.

This congregational exuberance was exciting. It energized my preaching. The congregation drew something new out of me. It helped me along, upholding me as I preached. It was easier and more rewarding than preaching to people who walk out, fall asleep, or look bored. Afterward, the other preachers teased me about when they first met me a year earlier and I seemed quiet and shy. "But now we know that you can preach."

A writer tells of the Good Friday service in his community where all the town's African-American congregations gather for three hours of preaching from their various pastors. One preacher was particularly good, and his successor had a difficult time.

> He was so unnerved by this task that he stammered through the first ten minutes of his sermon, despite the encouragement of his faithful followers scattered among the other worshipers.
>
> Suddenly, the preacher stopped in midsentence and pled with the entire congregation: "Gimme some hep! Ah need yo hep! Ah can't do dis without yor hep, please hep me now." A shot of adrenaline bolted the congregation out of its lethargy. They responded as though they had been asked to pull a drowning child from a lake. With loud "Amens," hand-clapping, and shouts of encouragement from all quarters, the preacher ventured on, but now far, far above his previous meager level of ability. It wasn't the best sermon that afternoon, but it was surely the most exciting. The preacher didn't preach that sermon; the congregation did. It became *their* sermon![1]

In such settings, *amen* is rich and powerful. It is a word that brings a response and accomplishes something. Unfortunately, in the congregations I am used to, the word *amen* is often empty and vain. Perhaps a worship leader says it at the end of her sermon. It has been reduced to no more than a punctuation mark. But *amen* is more than just a period to end a sentence. It is not just a stage direction to let us know we can relax and open our eyes because the prayer is finished.

When someone says "Amen" it does not mean we who are listening can heave a sigh of relief and think, "Thank heavens that ordeal, that long prayer, is over!" In fact, the word is not only for the leader of the worship. It belongs to the whole congregation. It is for all of us to share and use.

Amen in the Bible

The congregation's use of "Amen" is illustrated in 1 Chronicles 16:36. There the worship leader prays:

> "Blessed be the Lord, the God of Israel,
> from everlasting to everlasting."

The passage concludes: "Then all the people said 'Amen!' and praised the Lord."

The Hebrew root for *amen* is connected to words that connote faith and confidence. "To have faith, biblically, means more than holding to certain truths; it also implies a serene trust in a mysterious, ultimate sense of reality."[2]

Amen suggests being firm, established, and strong. In the Old Testament, the word shows that one accepts God's will and implies a commitment to that will. In the New Testament, *amen* is often a worshipful response and is found at the end of prayers (Rev. 5:14; Gal. 1:5; Eph. 3:21; 1 Tim. 1:17).

Since Jesus is the key example of divine obedience, he himself is called *Amen*: "the Amen, the faithful and true witness" (Rev. 3:14.). Jesus begins many of his sayings with the phrase "truly, truly," which literally means "amen, amen."

Saying Yes to God

The little word *Amen* has important implications for our faith. When we say *Amen* we say "Yes" to God. We endorse God's purposes and his will. It is to make a serious commitment. It is never just a ritual. *Amen* means "Yes."

God calls us to make our lives an *Amen* to his purposes as we say "Yes!" to God. *Amen* is never merely a passive "let it be." It is a resolute commitment to be involved with God's kingdom. It shows our assent to God and to his kingdom and his will. Our example is Jesus himself, the Great *Amen* who said "Yes" to God's loving involvement with humanity. "For in him every one of God's promises is a 'Yes.' For this reason it is through him that we say the 'Amen,' to the glory of God" (2 Cor. 1:20).

Jesus is the first *Amen*. Whenever we repeat that word, whether in prayers or sermons, we commit ourselves to God's purposes. Thus we must beware of saying the word too lightly. To say amen with all our heart means we will obey God. Uttered in the context of the Lord's Prayer, our *amen* means *we* will hallow God's name, be part of bringing in God's kingdom, do God's will, share in bringing daily bread to others, forgive the debts of others, not tempt others, and not do evil to others.

Amen, God Is Faithful

The word *amen* does not just have implications for us. It is also a confession about *God*. It reminds us that God is able and faithful. It reminds us that God is worthy and trustworthy. It teaches us that God will fulfill what he has promised.

To say *amen* reminds us that we can count on God at all times and in all things. When our lives show trust in God, then our lives proclaim *amen*. Through the changes, troubles, and turbulence of our lives, we can count on God. In prayer God reminds us he loves and cares for us. In prayer we hear again and again that Jesus is the great *Amen* and thus we can count on God.

During the Persian Gulf War, people I knew felt unprecedented anxiety. Precisely such panic convinces some people that war is necessary. Even in the midst of horrors that make us weep, we should not lose sight of God. We should look to Jesus, the great *Amen*. He is always reliable. "Jesus Christ is the same yesterday and today and forever" (Heb. 13:8).

During war crises, I fear for our souls and the souls of all those connected to war. Lies, hate, evil, revenge, and pious self-righteousness are more destructive than poison gases. We are easily overwhelmed by forces of fear, hatred, violence, and despair. "For our struggle is not against enemies of blood and flesh, but against the rulers, against the authorities, against the cosmic powers of this present darkness, against the spiritual forces of evil in the heavenly places" (Eph. 6:12).

During the Persian Gulf War, we heard much about sealed rooms in Israel. Each home and apartment designated a sealed room where they would be safe and protected from the horrible possibility of poison gases.

Our spirits need sealed rooms too. The world's persuasive forces threaten to overwhelm us with the belief that war is necessary and even good. Our spirits need sealed rooms where we look to God and can hear his still, small voice and his universal weeping amid all bombings and clamorings. Our heart's sealed rooms are constructed of prayer and worship, Bible reading, fellowship, and proclamation.

> Worship is the vital center of the life together. The Lord who is praised opens the eyes of believers to discern the spreading darkness. The discernment can be borne only because, through worship, His light shines all the brighter over against that darkness.[3]

In the sealed rooms of our spirituality, we learn to count on God. I take comfort from this evening prayer.

> Stay with us, Father of light, and protect us through the silent hours of this night; we are wearied by the changes of this passing world: may we rest in your eternal changelessness, for you are faithful and your love never varies, through Jesus Christ, your Son, our Lord. Amen.[4]

Walter Wangerin tells the story of an old African-American woman who was dying of cancer. Her travail was horrible. The children's choir from Wangerin's church paid her a visit. Her suffering struck them silent and they could not sing. But her warm and loving nature won them over. Her faith inspired them when she said,

> Babies, babies, we be in the hand of Jesus, old ones, young ones, and us and you together. Jesus, he hold us in his hand, and ain' no one goin' to snatch us out. Jesus, he don' never let one of us go. Never. Not ever. . . .[5]

Then the children could sing once more.

17

Let Us Pray

The Virtue of Repetition

Once I began this project, many people frankly told me that they were bored with the Lord's Prayer. It had been repeated so often at school and in public ceremonies that the prayer seemed empty and meaningless. This set me to wondering whether repetition itself might ever be valuable.

We tend to be suspicious of repetition and rote memorization. In his teaching on prayer, in the Sermon on the Mount where one version of the Lord's Prayer is found, Jesus warns *against* empty repetition. "When you are praying, do not heap up empty phrases as the Gentiles do; for they think that they will be heard because of their many words" (Matt. 6:7). Repetition does not make God more likely to hear us. But repetition *can* be helpful.

Children certainly love and appreciate repetition. Any rhyme, song, or story that sounded good once is worth repeating over and over. According to the practice of my preschooler, if a joke is funny once, it is funny three hundred times. Children love repetition, whereas adults like to experience continually new stimulation.

I noticed this once when we were visiting my parents during Christmas vacation. The children got permission to watch television. The Sharon, Lois, and Bram episode they were watching turned out to be one they had seen before. Surprisingly, they were happy about this. Somehow they know that even within the familiar there are new things to be learned.

There are a few television shows that I watch only two or three times a year. Inevitably, it seems, when I decide to watch a show I have not seen for two or three months, it is an episode I have already seen. I hate that, but my children do not mind at all, for they do not crave continual novelty.

Boredom is a particularly severe plague in our day. People of my generation have a low boredom threshold. We expect to be continually entertained and amused. Boredom is a major factor in job and marriage failures. We are quick to complain whenever there seems to be too much repetition in our lives. Therefore prayer and worship sometimes feel tedious to us.

Television deals directly with this problem. It employs a battery of technical gimmicks to catch and keep our attention. Such technical events include the cut, zoom, superimposition, voice-over, shift to another scene, background music, and change in perspective. All of these are unnatural. They do not happen in real life. Normal television contains eight to ten artificial technical events per minute, while commercials have as many as twenty to thirty per minute![1]

> Each technical event—each alteration of what would be natural imagery—is intended to keep your attention from waning as it might otherwise. The effect is to lure your attention forward like a mechanical rabbit teasing a greyhound. Each time you are about to relax your attention, another technical event keeps you attached.[2]

Without that continual changing and shifting, we might realize how bored we really are.

> Leaving the television set to go outdoors, or to have an ordinary conversation, becomes unsatisfying. One wants action! Life becomes boring, and television interesting, all as a result of a system of technical hypes.[3]

How can prayer ever compete with such gimmicks? We tire of the Lord's Prayer because we think we know and understand it. But memorizing something, knowing it by heart, is not necessarily enough. To listen to the Lord's Prayer or to say it once or occasionally is not enough. To hear something once or a few times means only superficial acquaintance, without much processing. But if we hear something again and again, it becomes ours to own, explore, and understand.

Many important things need to be done over and over in a way that takes discipline and commitment. The story is told that a woman rushed up to Fritz Kreisler, the world famous violinist. "Oh, Mr. Kreisler, I would give my life to play the violin as beautifully as you do." His response was simple and direct: "I did." To learn any trade, skill, or craft takes much practice, and practice means repetition. Musicians repeat their scales over and over throughout their lives as rehearsing leads to deeper knowledge and understanding.

James Raffan likes to canoe in the wilderness and offers this reflection.

> Wilderness journeying is superficially and fundamentally a repetitive process; you get up, you travel, you go to sleep, you get up, you travel, you go to sleep; and so on. But what elevates this circular and rather mundane process to the imagination is the fact that every time the journey melody is reiterated by the voice of another day, you hear new harmonies and become cognizant of new meaning and new understandings. The longer the journey, the more you listen, the richer the music, the richer the potential reward.[4]

Likewise, to be a Christian takes practice and some of this practice involves repetition. It takes practice to learn and relearn how to repent. Practice to learn how to give and share. Practice to learn how to live and act lovingly. The usual word for such practice is *discipline*.

Another word is *habits*, although that sometimes has bad connotations. But to grow as Christians means that we must develop Christian habits of prayer and Bible study, church attendance and fellowship, service and giving. Habits can be good.

> The great benefit of good spiritual habits is that they enable us to practice the presence of God objectively—by reading His Word, spending time in prayer, worshipping, observing the Sabbath—even when positive subjective feelings are not there.[5]

Many things only become more meaningful as we repeat them. Only then do they become more deeply ingrained. We saw this in the Introduction where we considered how the phrase "I love you" works and changes throughout life. Children and adults say the same thing but do not mean precisely the same thing. The phrase becomes richer through the years.

The same is true of the Lord's Prayer. We may have learned it at a young age, but we cannot immediately appreciate its depth, meaning, and richness. Jesus taught us these good words of prayer. We can pray these words even as we learn better how to pray it. Praying the Lord's Prayer is to spirituality what practicing the scales is to music.

When One Is Unable to Pray

It is not only that the Lord's Prayer (or indeed the Psalms or the great hymns for that matter) teach us to pray through their repetition. It is not only that they have meanings requiring constant exploring. There is at least one other virtue in such repetition. There are times in our lives when we do not know how to pray. There are times when we do not know what to pray about.

I remember January 16, 1991, when Allied forces began bombing Iraq. People in our congregation immediately called an emergency prayer meeting. We arrived at the church building sober and shocked. Several people said they were not sure *how* to pray or *what* we should pray for. But we prayed nevertheless. There were familiar prayers and new ones. We read Bible texts, some familiar and some new. The repetition of the old and familiar helped us to pray.

One friend told me that one day he found himself on a surgery table and wanted to pray but suddenly could not. Then he remembered a prayer he was taught in church and he prayed.

Another woman tells of the time she was having great difficulty with her twenty-year old son. Nothing she did ever seemed to succeed or get through to him. There never seemed to be any progress. She was deeply discouraged.

One day she brought him to the airport so he could return to his home. It had been a terrible visit with nothing resolved. She dropped him off and drove away. The situation felt absolutely hopeless. She wanted to cry and tried to pray but could not.

Suddenly she remembered a prayer she learned in church. A prayer that she had often repeated but had never really heard. And she prayed.

When I was a teenager, I used to roam the fields near our house after dark. I fervently spoke to and with God at great length, sometimes for hours. But after my sister died when I was twenty years old, I could not find the words to pray. Torn by grief and mourning, prayer did not come spontaneously. Since I had only learned about spontaneous prayer, I could no longer pray. It was only through discovering the resources of prayers like the Lord's Prayer and the Psalms that I learned again to pray.

A woman's eighty-one-year-old mother-in-law suffered a stroke. Her relatively independent life was irreversibly altered, and the family was forced to put her into a nursing home. There she lived for five years, never showing any emotion when her family visited. "A half smile was all that was left of the animated woman who only a few years ago used to pick strawberries and scramble up rocky cliffs by the seashore. Over the years we watched her slip further and further away."[6]

One New Year's Day, the whole family was gathered for celebrations. The old woman was brought home for the occasion, even though no one could possibly know what it might mean to her. The family gathered around the piano and began to sing Christmas carols

> and when they came to "Silent Night" I could hardly believe my ears. Mom was singing too. Her voice was soft, but she was on key and she knew the words. Everybody was stunned, but they kept on singing. They smiled at her and she nodded. They sang other carols and then went on to some of Mom's favorite hymns—"Amazing Grace," "What a Friend We Have in Jesus," "Holy, Holy, Holy." She sang them all.
>
> It was a moment of incredible warmth and joy, blessing and almost magical beauty. Even when she couldn't recognize the faces of her own children, even when she seemed incapable of laughter or tears, the songs of faith were still alive. Deep within her spirit, well below the frost line of illness and loss, the hymns survived.[7]

The Majestic Thunder of Mighty Waters

> The voice of the Lord is over the waters;
> the God of glory thunders,
> the Lord, over mighty waters.
> The voice of the Lord is powerful;
> the voice of the Lord is full of majesty. (Ps. 29:3-4)

> I saw one like the Son of man . . . and his voice was like the sound of many waters. (Rev. 1:13b, 15b)

One place where I always find myself able to pray is near bodies of water. The children and I often walk to a rock beach along the Detroit River. Our times together there often feel prayerful to me. Sometimes I take troubled people for walks along that very beach too. The environment is a healing one.

When the children and I go to the beach, we repeat ourselves a lot, doing the same things over and over. We walk the same route first of all. We explore and look around. Each visit, we examine their initials that I once carved into an old log. We throw lots of rocks into the river, trying to fill it up. Sometimes we skip rocks until our arms ache. And I do a lot of watching.

By the water, we have many habits. These repetitive habits do not bear immediate fruit, but they are not in vain. The kids never stop tossing rocks, but they do not accomplish anything. I have whiled away many an hour trying to build a sandcastle on another beach, only to have the wind and waves quickly erase my efforts. On vacations, I have spent hours or even days trying to catch minnows or crayfish. Why? Why spend hours in such compulsive, unproductive behavior?

Because I know that water is healing. Being beside or near water is calming and meditative. I don't know precisely why. Perhaps it is the changing colors, the lapping sound of the water, the rhythm of the waves where everything keeps changing but somehow remains the same. Perhaps it is the play of the sunlight on water. Or maybe just the fresh air.

I do know that many of my life's best moments have come by the water. In my first memory of my grandfather, I stand with him on a wooden bridge where we are fishing. I remember being a teenager when our family rented a cottage. On some mornings, I arose early and walked to the beach. There I prayed and wrote poetry. I thought of the things of God and dreamed of being a writer.

I remember wandering the shore of the Sea of Galilee and imagining Jesus there. I remember wading in the Mediterranean and the Gulf of Eilat. I think about birding by the water in Florida.

Or I remember the summer of 1982 when I lived in Elkhart, Indiana, and had a terrible experience of burn-out. Every day I went to a little park by a small river to read, pray, think, wade, and watch the antics of the ducks. I remember a quick visit to a Haiti beach in 1990, where the beauty of the scenery contrasted with the sufferings of that precious country.

Although the locations varied widely, they had much in common. All these times by the water were occasions of prayer, rest, inspiration, and peace. Each scene was different. But each was somehow the same—bound together by the power of the water, the rhythm of the waves, the massive unchangingness.

These water experiences are like the familiar prayers the Lord and the church have handed down to us. Each time I pray the Lord's Prayer, it is familiar to be sure. But it is also new every time. There are new depths, waves, rhythms, and implications.

We need to sit by the rivers of life God has poured out for us. To watch the rhythm of the waves. To smell the air. To be amused by the birds.

And to pray.

> But may all who seek you rejoice and be glad in you;
>   may those who love your salvation
>   say continually, "Great is the Lord!"
> As for me, I am poor and needy,
>   but the Lord takes thought for me.
> You are my help and my deliverer;
>   do not delay, O my God. (Ps. 40:16-17)

Study Guide

Introduction

1. Are you bored with the Lord's Prayer? Why? Do we repeat it too often?

2. Are you surprised that many historical church leaders valued the Lord's Prayer highly? Why? Why did they value the Lord's Prayer so much?

3. Discuss why you do or do not agree that the Lord's Prayer is a good model for all Christian prayer.

Chapter One

1. Which version of the Lord's Prayer do you prefer, Matthew's or Luke's?

2. Compare the two versions of the Lord's Prayer. Then contrast them with the way you traditionally pray the Lord's Prayer. What most surprises, disturbs, or pleases you?

3. How do *you* think the Lord's Prayer is organized and divided?

4. Should we show more respect for the holy uniqueness of the Lord's Prayer? If so, how might we do this?

Chapter Two

1. If our society has fallen into a destructive individualism, how can Christian prayer help recover God's priorities of community and mutual aid?

2. If "our" relationship to God is connected so closely with other people, can any of us correctly talk about "my personal relationship with Jesus"?

3. What are the practical and spiritual implications of calling God "*our* Father"?

4. How does prayer keep our spirits healthy?

Chapter Three

1. Have you had any trouble calling God "Father" in the Lord's Prayer?

2. How do you feel about substituting other titles for God in the Lord's Prayer?

3. How has the idea of God the Father been abused by human males?

4. Can the notion of God as Father call and challenge human fathers to deeper faithfulness and gentleness?

Chapter Four

1. What does the name "Father" imply about God's commitments to us?

2. How can trust in God's providence nurture a healthy spirituality?

3. How is obedience connected with our relationship with God?

Chapter Five

1. Why do we need to deal with God's distance or transcendence?

2. How does God overcome his transcendence to meet us on earth?

3. Do you agree that our generation tries to be too "chummy" with God?

Chapter Six

1. How and where have you noticed the importance of names?

2. Can you think of examples where a believer's familiarity with God ended up with God's name being taken in vain?

3. What are some of this chapter's important implications for evangelism?

Chapter Seven

1. Are you longing for God's kingdom? What are crises or problems that cause your longing?
2. Where do you see signs of the kingdom having arrived?
3. Where do you see signs that the kingdom still needs to arrive?

Chapter Eight

1. When you encounter a bad situation or unfortunate incident, does it comfort you to think "it must be God's will"?
2. When we pray for God's will to be done, what commitment are we making?
3. Why is obedience so central to Christian spirituality?

Chapter Nine

1. Do you agree that the little phrase "on earth as in heaven" is at the center of the Lord's Prayer? Why?
2. What are the important connections between heaven and earth?
3. How does God want heaven to affect the earth?

Chapter Ten

1. How does contemporary society make us dissatisfied with what we already have?
2. Can we North Americans pray "give us this day our daily bread" with integrity? Why?
3. Are you surprised that the Lord's Prayer, that exemplary model of all Christian prayers, talks about something as mundane as bread?

Chapter Eleven

1. How are we dependent on God?
2. How is our forgiveness accomplished? What does God actually forgive?

3. In the possible versions of the petition, do you prefer "sins," "debts," or "trespasses"? Why?

Chapter Twelve

1. Is God's forgiveness conditional on our forgiveness?
2. What are the hazards of comparing God's forgiveness to our forgiveness?
3. Does the Lord's Prayer have economic implications for us? If so, what are they?
4. In what ways does forgiveness set people free?

Chapter Thirteen

1. Many people are bothered by this petition. How do you understand it?
2. What are tests and temptations that the church faces today?
3. How does our society make us more vulnerable to temptation?

Chapter Fourteen

1. How is evil distinct from temptation?
2. How does Satan work through governments and institutions?
3. Where in your life can you identify with the despairing cry of panic, "deliver us from evil"?

Chapter Fifteen

1. Why is it appropriate to end this prayer with a doxology?
2. Why is there no doxology included in the Bible's versions of the Lord's Prayer?
3. What are practical implications of a worshipful doxology?

Chapter Sixteen

1. What does "amen" really mean? Has it become an empty formality for us?
2. What does the word "amen" teach us about God? About Jesus? Why is Jesus called the great Amen?
3. How can you recover the deep meaning of the word "Amen"?

Chapter Seventeen

1. How do you feel about the Lord's Prayer now?
2. Do you think that regularly repeating a familiar prayer could be helpful to spirituality? Why?
3. Where have you found yourself best able to pray?

Notes

Introduction

1. Dietrich Bonhoeffer, *The Cost of Discipleship* (London: SCM Press, 1959), p. 148.

2. Will Campbell, *God on Earth* (New York: Crossroad Pub. Co., 1983), p. 6.

3. Simone Weil, *Waiting for God,* trans. Emma Craufurd (New York: Harper & Row, 1951), p. 71.

4. Ibid., p. 227.

5. As quoted in James Houston, *The Transforming Friendship* (Batavia, Ill.: Lion Publishing Corporation, 1989), p. 166.

Chapter One

1. Leonardo Boff, *The Lord's Prayer,* trans. Theodore Morrow (Maryknoll, N.Y.: Orbis Books, 1983), pp. 4-5.

2. Ernst Lohmeyer, *The Lord's Prayer,* trans. John Bowden (London: Collins, 1965), p. 21.

3. Joachim Jeremias, *The Lord's Prayer,* trans. John Reumann (Philadelphia: Fortress Press, 1983), p. iii.

4. Lohmeyer, *The Lord's Prayer,* p. 14.

5. Houston, *The Transforming Friendship,* pp. 178.

6. Michael H. Crosby, O.F.M. Cap. *Thy Will Be Done: Praying the Our Father as Subversive Activity* (Maryknoll, N.Y.: Orbis Books, 1977), p. 2.

7. Gene L. Davenport, *Into the Darkness* (Nashville, Tenn.: Abingdon, 1988), pp. 202-203.

8. Jeremias, *The Lord's Prayer,* p. vi.

9. Crosby, *Thy Will Be Done,* pp. 2-3.

10. William Barclay, *The Plain Man Looks at the Lord's Prayer* (London: Collins, 1964), p. 19.

11. Timothy K. Jones, "What Can I Say?" *Christianity Today,* November 5, 1990, p. 26.

12. As quoted by Timothy K. Jones, "What Can I Say?" p. 29.

Chapter Two

1. Michael H. Crosby, O.F.M. Cap. *Thy Will Be Done: Praying the Our Father as Subversive Activity* (Maryknoll, N.Y.: Orbis Books, 1977).

2. Henri J. M. Nouwen, *Behold the Beauty of the Lord* (Notre Dame, Ind.: Ave Maria Press, 1987), p. 59.

3. Houston, *The Transforming Friendship,* p. 179.

4. Davenport, *Into the Darkness,* p. 201.

5. Boff, *The Lord's Prayer,* p. 28.

Chapter Three

1. Diane Tennis, *Is God the Only Reliable Father?* (Philadelphia: Westminster Press, 1985), Chapter Three.

2. Susanne Heine, *Matriarchs, Goddesses, and Images of God,* trans. John Bowden (Philadelphia: Augsburg, 1988), p. 38.

3. Ibid.

4. Adelia Neufeld Wiens, "Bushdance, Rough Shepherds and Generous Gifts," *Mennonite Reporter,* 1 October 1990, p. 15.

5. John W. Miller, *Biblical Faith and Fathering* (Mahwah, N.J.: Paulist Press, 1989), p. 110.

6. Ibid., p. 113.

7. Walter Wink, "The New RSV: The Best Translation, Halfway There," *Christian Century,* 19-26 September 1990, p. 832.

8. See Millard C. Lind, *Monotheism, Power, Justice* (Elkhart, Ind.: Institute of Mennonite Studies, 1990), p. 256.

9. Virginia Ramey Mollenkott, *The Divine Feminine* (New York: Crossroad, 1987).

10. Elizabeth Achtemeier, "The Impossible Possibility," *Interpretation,* January 1988, pp. 55-56.

11. Elizabeth Schussler Fiorenza, *In Memory of Her* (New York: Crossroad, 1989), p. 151. See also Willard M. Swartley, *Slavery, Sabbath, War, and Women* (Scottdale, Pa.: Herald Press, 1983), p. 164.

12. Willard M. Swartley, "God as Father: Patriarch or Paternity," in *Daughters of Sarah,* November/December 1990, p. 13.

13. Barclay, *The Plain Man Looks at the Lord's Prayer,* pp. 11-12.

14. Ibid., p. 32.

15. Eugene H. Peterson, *Reversed Thunder* (San Francisco: Harper & Row, 1988), p. 18.

16. ________, *Answering God* (San Francisco: Harper & Row, 1989), pp. 25-26.

17. Luke T. Johnson, *Faith's Freedom* (Minneapolis: Fortress Press, 1990) p. 101.

18. Diane Tennis, *Is God the Only Reliable Father*, p. 9.

Chapter Four

1. Henri J. M. Nouwen, *Making All Things New* (San Francisco: Harper & Row, 1981), pp. 25-28.

2. *The Heidelberg Catechism* (Philadelphia: United Church Press, 1962), Question 120, p. 119.

3. William O'Brien, "Philip Berrigan and Elizabeth McAlister," *The Other Side*, May/June 1989, pp. 12-18.

4. George MacDonald, *The Maiden's Bequest*, ed. Michael R. Phillips (Minneapolis: Bethany House Publishers, 1985), pp. 105-106.

5. Lohmeyer, *The Lord's Prayer*, pp. 45-46.

6. Houston, *The Transforming Friendship*, p. 176.

7. James Lee Burke, *The Neon Rain* (New York: Henry Holt and Co., 1987), pp. 180-181.

Chapter Five

1. Douglas V. Steere, *Intercession* (Cincinnati: Forward Movement Publications), 1989, p. 1.

2. Ibid., p. 5.

3. Ibid., pp. 5-6.

4. Thomas Merton, *Bread in the Wilderness* (New York: New Directions Books, 1953), p. 43.

5. Boff, *The Lord's Prayer*, p. 32.

6. Davenport, *Into the Darkness*, p. 208.

7. Mid-day Office, Taizé Community, *The Oxford Book of Prayer*, ed. George Appleton (Oxford: Oxford University Press, 1985), p. 186.

Chapter Six

1. Weil, *Waiting for God*, p. 216.

2. George MacDonald, *The Highlander's Last Song*, ed. Michael R. Phillips (Minneapolis: Bethany House Publishers, 1986), pp. 113-114.

3. Eugene C. Roehlkepartain, "Shopping for the Ultimate in Jesuswear," *The Christian Century*, September 5-12, 1990, p. 788-789.

4. As quoted in *The Other Side*, July/August 1987, p. 43.

5. Howard Zinn, *A People's History of the United States* (New York: Harper & Row, 1980), pp. 305-306.

6. Zinn, *A People's History of the United States*, p. 309.

7. Davenport, *Into the Darkness*, p. 211.

8. Walker Percy, "Notes for a Novel About the End of the World," in *The Failure and the Hope*, eds. Will D. Campbell and James Y. Holloway (Grand Rapids, Mich.: Eerdmans, 1972), p. 240.

9. Frederick Buechner, *The Magnificent Defeat* (New York: Seabury Press, 1980), p. 111.

10. Clarence Jordan, *The Substance of Faith,* ed. Dallas Lee (New York: Association Press, 1972), pp. 134-135.

11. Barclay, *The Plain Man Looks at the Lord's Prayer,* pp. 57-58.

12. As quoted in Barclay, p. 60.

Chapter Seven

1. Alan Rayburn, "How Canada Lost Its 'Dominion,' " *Canadian Geographic,* June/July 1990, pp. 86-87.

2. Gordon MacDonald, *Forging Real World Faith* (Nashville, Tenn.: Oliver Nelson, 1989), p. 93.

3. "Departure-zone Hostage Sets His Sights on . . . Anywhere!" Reuter Story, *Windsor Star,* Thursday, July 12, 1990, p. A1.

4. Bonhoeffer, *The Cost of Discipleship,* p. 148.

Chapter Eight

1. Davenport, *Into the Darkness,* p. 216.

2. Ibid., p. 217.

3. Dom Hélder Câmara, *Through the Gospel with Dom Hélder Câmara,* trans. Alan Neame (Maryknoll, N.Y.: Orbis Books, 1986), p. 58.

4. *Mennonite Encyclopedia,* Vol. II (Scottdale, Pa.: Herald Press, 1956), p. 448.

5. Ibid.

6. Ibid., p. 449.

7. Ibid.

Chapter Nine

1. Lohmeyer, *The Lord's Prayer,* p. 113.

2. Boff, *The Lord's Prayer,* p. 72.

3. Ibid. p. 72.

4. Lohmeyer, *The Lord's Prayer,* p. 126.

5. Frederick Buechner, *Wishful Thinking* (New York: Harper & Row, 1973), p. 84.

6. Søren Kierkegaard, *Purity of Heart Is to Will One Thing,* trans. Douglas V. Steere (New York: Harper & Row, 1948), p. 79.

7. As quoted by Walter Brueggemann, *Israel's Praise* (Philadelphia: Fortress Press, 1988), p. 131.

8. John K. Stoner and Lois Barrett, *Letters to American Christians* (Scottdale, Pa.: Herald Press, 1989), p. 114.

9. Al Alvarez, *Feeding the Rat* (London: Bloomsbury, 1988), p. 84.

10. Ibid., p. 71.

Chapter Ten

1. Michael Harrington, *The Other America* (New York: Viking Penguin, 1962, 1971).

2. William A. Dyrness, *Learning About Theology from the Third World* (Grand Rapids: Zondervan, 1990), p. 62.

3. Ibid., pp. 62-63.

4. Marshall Shelly, "Within a Leader's Soul, Ambition and Contentment Must Coexist in Peace," *Leadership*, Summer 1990, p. 3.

5. Boff, *The Lord's Prayer*, pp. 75-76.

6. Ibid., p. 75.

7. Ibid., p. 85.

8. *The Times-Picayune*, Wed., May 2, 1990, p. B-4.

9. David Bottoms, *Easter Weekend* (New York: Houghton Mifflin, 1990), p. 56.

10. Quoted by Barclay, *The Plain Man Looks at the Lord's Prayer*, pp. 95-96.

11. Boff, *The Lord's Prayer*, p. 77.

12. Davenport, *Into the Darkness*, p. 224.

13. Quoted in Boff, *The Lord's Prayer*, p. 84.

14. Deborah Kay Bragg, "Daily Bread," *The Other Side*, July/August 1988, p. 17.

15. Carroll B. Houle, Maryknoll article quoted in *The Other Side*, November 1987, p. 9.

Chapter Eleven

1. Lohmeyer, *The Lord's Prayer*, p. 178.

2. Anonymous, "A.A. and the Church: A Comparison," *Urban Connections*, December 1988, p. 5.

3. Philip Yancey, *I Was Just Wondering* (Grand Rapids, Mich.: Eerdmans, 1989), p. 45.

4. Ibid., p. 43.

5. Ibid., p. 44.

6. As quoted by Brennan Manning, *The Ragamuffin Gospel* (Portland Ore.: Multnomah, 1990), p. 1.

7. Karl Barth, *Prayer*, ed. Don E. Saliers and trans. Sara F. Terrien (Philadelphia, Pa.: Westminster Press, 1985), p. 74.

8. JoAnn Ford Watson, "Steps of Forgiveness," *Pulpit Digest*, March/April 1989, p. 42.

9. Jan Milic Lochman, *The Lord's Prayer*, trans. Geoffrey Bromiley (Grand Rapids, Mich.: Eerdmans, 1990), pp. 120-121.

10. Dudley Fitts, ed., *Herbert* (New York: Dell Publishing Co., 1962), pp. 176-177.

Chapter Twelve

1. Jeremias, *The Lord's Prayer*, p. 27.

2. Buechner, *Wishful Thinking,* p. 28.

3. Barth, *Prayer,* p. 76.

4. John Howard Yoder, *The Politics of Jesus* (Grand Rapids, Mich.: Eerdmans, 1972), p. 66.

5. Buechner, *Wishful Thinking,* pp. 28-29.

6. Jeremias, *The Lord's Prayer,* p. 28.

7. Thomas Merton, *The Hidden Ground of Love,* ed. William H. Shannon (New York: Farrar, Straus, Giroux, 1985), p. 141.

8. Thomas R. Yoder-Neufeld, *Forgiveness and the Dangerous Few: The Biblical Basis,* unpublished paper, p. 7.

9. As quoted in James F. Drane, "Karl A. Menninger: Psychiatrist as Moralist," *Christian Century,* August 22-29, 1990, p. 759.

Chapter Thirteen

1. Lohmeyer, *The Lord's Prayer,* p. 198.

2. Davenport, *Into the Darkness,* p. 232.

Chapter Fourteen

1. Quoted by Timothy K. Jones, "The Devil Who is There," *Christianity Today,* August 20, 1990, p. 15.

2. M. Scott Peck, M.D., *People of the Lie* (New York: Simon and Schuster, 1983).

3. Ibid., p. 51.

4. Ibid., pp. 51-52. Emphasis added.

5. Ibid., p. 53.

6. Ibid., p. 56.

7. Ibid., p. 57.

8. Barth, *Prayer,* p. 84.

9. Quoted by Timothy K. Jones, "Frederick Buechner's Sacred Journey," *Christianity Today,* October 8, 1990, p. 51.

Chapter Fifteen

1. Elizabeth Abbot, *Haiti* (Toronto: McGraw-Hill Company, 1988), p. 132.

2. John Alexander, "The Fear of God," *The Other Side,* January/February 1989, p. 48.

3. As quoted in Kathryn Spink, *Jean Vanier and L'Arche* (Nepean, Ont.: Meakin and Associates, 1990), p. 201.

4. Robert Fulghum, *All I Really Need to Know I Learned in Kindergarten* (New York: Villard Books, 1989), p. 192.

5. Buechner, *Wishful Thinking,* p. 30.

6. Alexander, "The Fear of God," p. 48.

7. Barclay, *The Plain Man Looks at the Lord's Prayer,* p. 128.

Chapter Sixteen

1. Craig Douglas Erickson, *Participating in Worship* (Louisville: Westminster/John Knox Press, 1989), p. 32.

2. Boff, *The Lord's Prayer,* pp. 121-122.

3. Dale Aukerman, *Darkening Valley* (New York: The Seabury Press, 1981), p. 203.

4. *Praise God: Common Prayer at Taizé,* trans. Emily Chisholm (New York: Oxford University Press, 1977), p. 225.

5. Walter Wangerin, Jr., *The Manger is Empty* (San Francisco: Harper & Row, Publishers, 1989), p. 9.

Chapter Seventeen

1. Jerry L. Mander, *Four Arguments for the Elimination of Television* (New York: Quill, 1978), p. 308.

2. Ibid., p. 303.

3. Ibid., p. 304.

4. James Raffan, *Summer North of Sixty* (Toronto: Key Porter Books, 1990), p. ix.

5. Marva J. Dawn, *Keeping the Sabbath Wholly,* p. 208.

6. Sarah S. Miller, "Below the Frost Line, Hymns of Faith," *Christian Century,* December 12, 1990, p. 1157.

7. Ibid., pp. 1157-1158.

Bibliography

Abbot, Elizabeth. *Haiti*. Toronto: McGraw-Hill Company, 1988.

Achtemeier, Elizabeth. "The Impossible Possibility," *Interpretation*. January 1988, pp. 45-57.

Alexander, John. "The Fear of God," *The Other Side*. January/February 1989, pp. 47-48.

Alvarez, Al. *Feeding the Rat*. London: Bloomsbury, 1988.

Anonymous, "A.A. and the Church: A Comparison," *Urban Connections*, December 1988, pp. 4-5.

Appleton, George, ed. *The Oxford Book of Prayer*. Oxford: Oxford University Press, 1985.

Aukerman, Dale. *Darkening Valley*. Scottdale, Pa.: Herald Press, 1989.

Barclay, William. *The Plain Man Looks at the Lord's Prayer*. London: Collins, 1964.

Barth, Karl. *Prayer*. Ed. Don E. Saliers. Trans. Sara F. Terrien. Philadelphia: Westminster Press, 1985.

Boff, Leonardo. *The Lord's Prayer*. Trans. Theodore Morrow. Maryknoll, N.Y.: Orbis Books, 1983.

Bonhoeffer, Dietrich. *The Cost of Discipleship*. London: SCM Press, 1959.

Bottoms, David. *Easter Weekend*. New York: Houghton Mifflin, 1990.

Bragg, Deborah Kay. "Daily Bread," *The Other Side*. July/August 1988, p. 17.

Brueggemann, Walter. *Israel's Praise*. Philadelphia: Fortress Press, 1988.

Buechner, Frederick. *The Magnificent Defeat*. New York: Seabury Press, 1966.

____________. *Wishful Thinking*. New York: Harper & Row, 1973.

Burke, James Lee. *The Neon Rain*. New York: Henry Holt and Co., 1987.

Câmara, Dom Hélder. *Through the Gospel with Dom Hélder Câmara*. Trans. Alan Neame. Maryknoll, N.Y.: Orbis Books, 1986.

Campbell, Will. *God on Earth*. New York: Crossroad, 1983.

Crosby, Michael H., OFM Cap. *Thy Will Be Done: Praying the Our Father as Subversive Activity*. Maryknoll, N.Y.: Orbis Books, 1977.

Davenport, Gene L. *Into the Darkness*. Nashville, Tenn.: Abingdon, 1988.

Drane, James F. "Karl A. Menninger: Psychiatrist as Moralist," *Christian Century*. August 22-29, 1990, p. 759.

Dyrness, William A. *Learning About Theology from the Third World*. Grand Rapids, Mich.: Zondervan, 1990.

Erickson, Craig Douglas. *Participating in Worship*. Louisville, Ky.: Westminster/ John Knox Press, 1989.

Fiorenza, Elizabeth Schussler. *In Memory of Her*. New York: Crossroad, 1989.

Fulghum, Robert. *All I Really Need to Know I Learned in Kindergarten*. New York: Villard Books, 1989.

The Heidelberg Catechism. Philadelphia: United Church Press, 1962

Heine, Susanne. *Matriarchs, Goddesses, and Images of God*. Trans. John Bowden. Philadelphia: Augsburg, 1988.

Houston, James. *The Transforming Friendship*. Batavia Ill.: Lion Publishing Corporation, 1989.

Jeremias, Joachim. *The Lord's Prayer*. Trans. John Reumann. Philadelphia: Fortress Press, 1983.

____________. *The Prayers of Jesus*. Trans. John Bowden. Philadelphia: Fortress Press, 1967.

Johnson, Luke T. *Faith's Freedom*. Minneapolis: Fortress Press, 1990.

Jones, Timothy K. "The Devil Who Is There," *Christianity Today*. August 20, 1990, p. 15.

____________. "Frederick Buechner's Sacred Journey," *Christianity Today*. October 8, 1990, pp. 51-54

____________. "What Can I Say?" *Christianity Today*. November 5, 1990, pp. 26-29.

Jordan, Clarence. *The Substance of Faith*. Ed. Dallas Lee. New York: Association Press, 1972.

Kierkegaard, Søren. *Purity of Heart Is to Will One Thing*. Trans. Douglas V. Steere. New York: Harper & Row, 1948.

Lind, Millard C. *Monotheism, Power, Justice*. Elkhart, Ind.: Institute of Mennonite Studies, 1990.

Lochman, Jan Milic. *The Lord's Prayer*. Trans. Geoffrey Bromiley. Grand Rapids, Mich.: Eerdmans, 1990.

Lohmeyer, Ernst. *The Lord's Prayer*. Trans. John Bowden. London: Collins, 1965.

MacDonald, George. *The Highlander's Last Song*. Ed. Michael R. Phillips. Minneapolis: Bethany House Publishers, 1986.

________________. *The Maiden's Bequest*. Ed. Michael R. Phillips. Minneapolis: Bethany House Publishers, 1985.

MacDonald, Gordon. *Forging Real World Faith*. Nashville, Tenn.: Oliver Nelson, 1989.

Mander, Jerry L. *Four Arguments for the Elimination of Television*. New York: Quill, 1978.

Manning, Brennan. *The Ragamuffin Gospel*. Portland, Ore.: Multnomah, 1990.

Merton, Thomas. *Bread in the Wilderness*. New York: New Directions Books, 1953.

________________. *The Hidden Ground of Love*. Ed. William H. Shannon. New York: Farrar, Straus, Giroux, 1985.

Miller, John W. *Biblical Faith and Fathering*. Mahwah, N.J.: Paulist Press, 1989.

Miller, Sarah S. "Below the Frost Line, Hymns of Faith," *Christian Century*. December 12, 1990, pp. 1157-1158.

Mollenkott, Virginia Ramey. *The Divine Feminine*. New York: Crossroad, 1987.

Nouwen, Henri J. M. *Behold the Beauty of the Lord*. Notre Dame, Ind.: Ave Maria Press, 1987.

________________. *Making All Things New*. San Francisco: Harper & Row, 1981.

O'Brien, William. "Philip Berrigan and Elizabeth McAlister." *The Other Side*, May/June 1989, pp. 12-18.

Peck, M. Scott. *People of the Lie*. New York: Simon and Schuster, 1983.

Percy, Walker. "Notes for a Novel About the End of the World," in *The Failure and the Hope*. Eds. Will D. Campbell and James Y. Holloway. Grand Rapids, Mich.: Eerdmans, 1972.

Peterson, Eugene H. *Answering God*. San Francisco: Harper & Row, 1989.

________________. *Reversed Thunder*. San Francisco: Harper & Row, 1988.

Praise God: Common Prayer at Taizé. Trans. Emily Chisholm. New York: Oxford University Press, 1977.

Raffan, James. *Summer North of Sixty*. Toronto: Key Porter Books, 1990.

Rayburn, Alan. "How Canada Lost Its 'Dominion,' " *Canadian Geographic*. June/July 1990, pp. 86-87.

Roehlkepartain, Eugene C. "Shopping for the Ultimate in Jesuswear," *The Christian Century*. September 5-12, 1990.

Shelly, Marshall. "Within a Leader's Soul, Ambition and Contentment Must Coexist in Peace," *Leadership*. Summer 1990.

Spink, Kathryn. *Jean Vanier and L'Arche*. Nepean, Ont.: Meakin and Associates, 1990.

Steere, Douglas V. *Intercession*. Cincinnati, Ohio: Forward Movement Publications, 1989.

Stoner, John K., and Lois Barrett. *Letters to American Christians*. Scottdale, Pa.: Herald Press, 1989.

Swartley, Willard M. "God As Father: Patriarchy or Paternity," *Daughters of Sarah*. November/December 1990.

________________. *Slavery, Sabbath, War, and Women*. Scottdale, Pa.: Herald Press, 1983.

Tennis, Diane. *Is God the Only Reliable Father?* Philadelphia: Westminster Press, 1985.

Wangerin, Jr., Walter. *The Manger is Empty*. San Francisco: Harper & Row, Publishers, 1989.

Watson, JoAnn Ford. "Steps of Forgiveness," *Pulpit Digest*. March/April 1989.

Weil, Simone. *Waiting for God*. Trans. Emma Craufurd. New York: Harper & Row, 1951.

Wiens, Adelia Neufeld. "Bushdance, Rough Shepherds and Generous Gifts," *Mennonite Reporter*. 1 October 1990.

Wink, Walter. "The New RSV: The Best Translation, Halfway There," *Christian Century*, 19-26 September 1990.

Yancey, Philip. *I Was Just Wondering*. Grand Rapids, Mich.: Eerdmans: 1989.

Yoder, John Howard. *The Politics of Jesus*. Grand Rapids, Mich.: Eerdmans, 1972.

Yoder-Neufeld, Thomas R. *Forgiveness and the Dangerous Few: The Biblical Basis*, unpublished paper.

Zinn, Howard. *A People's History of the United States*. New York: Harper & Row, 1980.

Scripture Index

The Author

Arthur Paul Boers is a Mennonite pastor in Ontario.

He is the author of *On Earth As in Heaven* (Herald Press, 1991) and *Justice That Heals* (Faith and Life Press, 1992). A freelance writer, he has had two hundred articles and reviews published in more than a dozen periodicals, including *Christian Living, Christian Ministry, Christianity Today, Gospel Herald, The Mennonite, Mennonite Reporter, Our Family, St. Anthony Messenger, Sojourners,* and *The Windsor Star*. He is a contributing editor for *The Other Side*, a columnist for both *Christian Living* and *Christian Ministry*, and received an award from the Evangelical Press Association.

The first child of Dutch immigrants, he was born in Ontario and joined a Mennonite congregation at age nineteen. He received a B.A. from the University of Western Ontario, where he majored in philosophy (1976-1979); an M.A. in peace studies from Mennonite Biblical Seminary (1981-1983); and an M.Div. from McCormick Theological Seminary (1985-1988).

In 1980, he married Lorna Jean McDougall. They have two children, Erin Margaret (1984) and Paul Edward (1987). Boers enjoys reading, birding, and the blues.